AN UNDISCOVERED
LIGHTHOUSE

AN UNDISCOVERED LIGHTHOUSE

NAVIGATING MY COMPLEX
RELATIONSHIP WITH ALCOHOL

SKY LUCAS

NEW DEGREE PRESS
COPYRIGHT © 2023 SKY LUCAS
All rights reserved.

AN UNDISCOVERED LIGHTHOUSE
Navigating My Complex Relationship With Alcohol

ISBN   979-8-88926-668-6   *Paperback*
              979-8-88926-669-3   *Ebook*

Table of Contents

AUTHOR'S NOTE		9
CHAPTER 1.	THE FIRST TIME	15
CHAPTER 2.	YOU CAN'T LOVE YOURSELF AND HATE YOUR EXPERIENCES	21
CHAPTER 3.	A CLUB FIGHT	35
CHAPTER 4.	SPIRAL	47
CHAPTER 5.	BROKEN COMMITMENTS	57
CHAPTER 6.	MICHAEL'S HERO'S JOURNEY	63
CHAPTER 7.	LIGHT IN DARK SPACES	71
CHAPTER 8.	KC—LIKE I WOULD DESSERT	75
CHAPTER 9.	NO	87
CHAPTER 10.	ALCOHOL AND RELATIONSHIPS	99
CHAPTER 11.	MILES—LEARNING COMPASSION	107
CHAPTER 12.	THE ABSTINENCE MYTH	121
CHAPTER 13.	LOST IN MOVEMENT	131
CONCLUSION		139
ACKNOWLEDGMENTS		145
APPENDIX		151

Author's Note

A year ago, I was on Instagram when I came across a book entitled *Quit Like a Woman: The Radical Choice to Not Drink in a Culture Obsessed with Alcohol,* written by Holly Whitaker. This book immediately drew me in, as I've considered the possibility of becoming sober, quitting drinking, or at the very least, decreasing my consumption, especially as I got older. I purchased the book on Amazon, received it two days later, and devoured it. Only a chapter in, a flood of negative, scary, and regretful memories came rushing in. I realized the words I read spoke directly to me.

The book told the stories of a woman who had (ab)used alcohol at different times in her life and had uncomfortable, sometimes painful, and shameful experiences. I had been there. The author described with openness and vulnerability the details of her personal trials and tribulations with alcohol and how it left her on her knees repeatedly. She echoed experiences I have had throughout my life. The drunken fights that leave you dizzy. Bad decisions from having too many shots of Jameson. A lack of accountability and productivity because of a string of hangovers, weekend after weekend. The list goes on.

As I continued reading, I realized many of our experiences were parallel. However, the author had taken a strong and direct approach to sobriety as the one and only answer. I racked my brain to think of other books and podcasts I have listened to regarding alcohol consumption and realized the polarity of sobriety and complete abstinence as the ultimate end goal. But what if there is not one end goal for everyone? What if it is not one-size-fits-all?

When I first set out to write this book, I was eager, excited, and daunted all at once to open up the conversation about alcohol and the possibility of managing a healthy relationship with it. I have had a long and complex relationship with alcohol throughout my life, so it is a topic I am drawn to. I have found myself searching for the topic of alcohol in conversations, communities, and content. I have listened to podcasts, watched YouTube videos, and read books about the topic of alcohol, but I kept coming across similar content and the same narrative—horror stories of alcoholism leading to sobriety and complete abstinence. Even though abstaining from alcohol for periods of time has crossed my mind more than once, I honestly could not see myself obtaining this ultimate goal of being sober in perpetuity.

I have these stories about my journey with alcohol since I started drinking at the age of fifteen. I have learned from these experiences and stories immensely. But what if I am currently rewriting my relationship with alcohol? And what if that does not end with sobriety? Does that mean my story is less important? Is there a world where I can attain a healthy and sustainable relationship with alcohol? Within these questions I found my why for sharing my story. This was when I knew this changing, multidimensional, scary, beautiful, and complex story that is my own with alcohol is worth sharing. Though continuing to evolve, it could serve as a lighthouse for anyone searching for themselves in a story like mine.

In the months to follow, I spoke to friends, people I work and have worked with, and family members to get a feel for their thoughts on the topic. What surprised me was the number of people willing to share in these conversations, and the stories they had that connected dots between us. The common thread I heard repeatedly was that everyone felt they could drink less, wanted to create more boundaries with alcohol consumption, and wanted to find a balance with drinking. Mostly everyone I spoke to had the ultimate goal of maintaining a healthy relationship with alcohol.

As I looked outside my circle, I found a substantial part of our society is overdrinking. According to an article in *Newsweek*,

"In a study of more than 34,000 adults, researchers found that 40 percent of American adults consume excessive amounts of alcohol and continue to do so" (Andrew, 2018).

As we have seemingly come out of the pandemic, we can't forget about the stress that led to many people who found themselves drinking more than ever before. During the pandemic, an article in *USA Today* said,

"Nearly one in five Americans were consuming an unhealthy amount of alcohol. Several studies have suggested Americans are buying more alcohol and drinking more frequently during the coronavirus pandemic" (Hauck, 2021).

Needless to say, there are enough people who have and still struggle with alcohol consumption and could use dialogue surrounding drinking moderation and attaining a healthy relationship with alcohol. Maybe there is a path for them that does not involve complete sobriety. I cannot discount that everyone *is* different, and as I have heard, read, and seen, for some, sobriety really is the only way. What I am challenging is that sobriety is the only way. For some, cutting down and moderation works, and for others practicing being soberish works. Ultimately it does not have to be one-size-fits-all. I have not and will not claim to have it all figured out. The truth is some days I feel like I have a grip on my alcohol consumption and other days I feel like I need to redirect my path. I am the embodiment of a work in progress, and I have learned *that is okay.*

At times in the process of writing this book, I felt that since I do not always feel I have attained the perfect homeostasis when it comes to alcohol, I'm unqualified to tell my story. But who is more qualified to share my story than me? I have lived to tell many of my experiences, which you can dig into as you read this book. Those stories will tell how I got to where I am today and hopefully paint a picture that it is not about reaching an end-all destination of perfection or being infallible. It is about figuring out the way that works for you, the way that you will work, and what best serves you. Maybe that is complete abstinence and maybe not.

I hope this sparks the flame to figure out the right path for you. I believe this is a shared conversation many of us are having with ourselves in this day and age. I feel compelled to open that up by sharing my own experiences in a real, raw, and unabridged way. How much more informed and educated would we be about alcohol and consumption if we took these inner conversations and shared them with each other without fear of judgment and criticism? This has affirmed my purpose in writing this book and sharing my voice, and I hope it moves you to keep reading.

For anyone out there who is dealing with a complicated relationship with alcohol, for anyone looking to find themselves within real stories about life lessons, alcohol, and growth, and for anyone struggling to be honest with themselves and others about storms they are dealing with, this book is for you.

CHAPTER 1:

The First Time

The first time I drank alcohol, I got *drunk*. When I say drunk, I mean full throttle, head first in the cavity, with no reservations drunk. At the time, I was fifteen years old, and my desire to experience and feel things fully was stronger than any logic I had. See, I was raised by what I thought were very strict parents. I came from a religious household with particular rules and boundaries around everything—from boys and what I could and could not wear to who I could be friends with and to what school functions I could attend. For much of my early youth, I abided by these boundaries, and then my curiosity and yearning to be free took aggressive hold. I started finding devious ways to do whatever I wanted.

On a humid Friday summer night, my childhood best friend Arianna and I planned to go to a school fair. We knew we had only a handful of hours before we had to clock back in at home for curfew. That certainly didn't stop us from going to a local liquor store and asking a seedy-looking man to buy us a bottle of cheap brandy. And, of course, we chugged it before heading into the fair and threw caution to the wind.

After fifteen years, I can still remember the heaviness and warmth vibrating through my body when we got there and met up with some friends who were also drinking. The entire time we were at the fair felt like ten minutes—a wild, carefree whirlwind. I vividly remember a song coming on, and I started dancing around tons of people, not feeling self-conscious or worried about anything. I met new people and talked to what seemed like everyone. I was laughing hysterically—the kind that makes your stomach hurt—having the time of my life. The details from our time at the fair are blurry, but I do remember feeling free. Mission accomplished.

Moments escaped me. Before I knew it, the alarm on my phone was ringing—the one I had set so we could remember it was time to head home. "Holy shit! We have to go. It's time," I anxiously screamed at Arianna.

Both my friend and I were still *very* drunk and in no way, shape, or form equipped to interact with her parents waiting for us at her house. Regardless we had to get home soon.

We walked to her car, wobbly and discombobulated. This was it. She was going to drive us home drunk. We did not talk about it or even weigh our options. We just accepted it as the next step in this night of freedom.

Luckily, and by the grace of God, we made it to her house unscathed. Her parents were already in bed, so we could sneak into her room quietly and pass out before anyone could tell how messed up we were. The rest of the night could have looked entirely different had they been up. Had we had an accident on our way home, the night could have ended in complete disaster. It all could have gone to shit or worse. I still think about this.

The next morning, I woke up to what would be the first of many, many, *many* hangovers. Death felt like it was upon me. Sweaty, shaky, and beyond exhausted, it felt like a semitruck smashed into my head, like it was going to disintegrate into smithereens. Even worse than the aggressive hangover, I had to act like I was totally fine once I got home. I could *not* let my parents suspect that I had gotten almost blackout drunk the night before.

Before Arianna dropped me off at home later that day, we got a call from our friend, who had also been drinking at the fair. She was hysterical, and we could barely understand what she was saying. Once we finally got her calmed down, she told us they had been in a car accident on their way home from the fair. The accident totaled our friend's car and injured one of them. Thank goodness that was the worst of it, and no one else received serious injuries.

I could feel this hollow pit in my stomach for hours after we hung up the call. *That could have been us. What if we hurt someone on the road? What if, what if?* I kept replaying it in my mind. Suddenly, this feeling of freedom did not feel quite as liberating as it had the night before.

Arianna and I didn't exchange words after that call. I think we both felt the same things: shock, fear, and regret. I went home later that day feeling like I had had my first real adult experience, which came with big consequences and heavy reflection. Arianna had driven us home the night before without hesitation, and I let her. I let her drive us home without asking her if she was okay even though I knew she wasn't. The reality was dawning on me, and I clearly saw I could easily ruin my life in the span of one night with something almost everyone I knew partook in.

I heard stories about teenagers who lost their lives in car crashes due to drunk driving. I knew of girls who had gotten drunk and were taken advantage of, or people who had an accident and got severely injured. But as naive as it sounds, I truthfully never believed anything like that could happen to me or my friends—a thought that would prove to be a detriment to my life going forward.

Looking back now, I wish I could shake my fifteen-year-old self and tell her if she does not learn from that lesson, she will continue having close calls until she starts to feel the direct impact of her choices with alcohol. I wish I could stop her from experiencing the pain, embarrassment, shame, and heaviness she would eventually endure because of drinking. I also wish I could tell you that night made me table my drinking and go on to live a safe and fun teenage life. But as you may have already gathered, that is not how I decided to write the rest of my story with alcohol.

This would be one of many bad nights and even worse morning-afters that would shape my life and form this very complex and layered relationship with alcohol. As I write this fifteen years later, I would love it if I could tell you that I have it figured out and that I haven't drank in years. That's not my reality.

I can say I am actually learning all these years later the catastrophic and life-altering consequences alcohol can have on my life. I am learning how important it is to be introspective, intentional, and careful with my alcohol consumption. And to challenge the ways society treats and views drinking. I am learning, fine-tuning, and carving out the path that looks right for me. Like I said or *warned you*, this is just one of a multitude of stories of mine I will share that may rock you to your core as they have me. So, buckle up.

CHAPTER 2:

You Can't Love Yourself and Hate Your Experiences

When I first decided to write this book, I knew I would have to relive the stories I have decided to share. I knew I would embark on a journey confronting and explaining emotions I have tucked away deep into my past.

This story, in particular, happened almost fifteen years ago and is the most traumatic, dismantling, and core-shaking thing I have ever had to live through. I hope this intro can serve as a trigger warning, as the story that follows has very sensitive material I am admittedly nervous about sharing.

I have gone back and forth as to whether this story was necessary to share or not. However, after much introspection, I find it essential to the grand tapestry that is my life, which has molded me into the woman I am today. You can't share just select parts of your truth. And if you feel compelled and are brave enough to share it, share it all. I have repeated that to myself while writing this entire book, and it is my ultimate hope you experience that as you read about my journey.

Waking up in a hospital bed without knowing how I got there has to be one of the scariest, most unnerving, and fragile moments I have had to experience. When I found out how I had gotten there has to be the first. On Saturday, around five-thirty in the morning, I came to. I was in a cold, dimly lit hospital room with a woman who had kind eyes sitting across from the bed I was in. She came right to my bedside and told me everything was going to be okay to keep me from panicking. After moments of silence between us, as I tried to collect myself, she asked me if I remembered anything that had happened the night prior. She wore regular clothes, so I knew she was not a nurse. And she looked at me with so much compassion I knew whatever I could not remember was not good.

"What happened?" I asked, still not coherent. "I don't remember! Are my parents here? Am I here alone? What hospital is this?" Hysterical and in shock, I remember barely being able to make out full sentences because of the sheer panic. It is a wonder she understood anything I was saying. "Who are you? How did I get here?" I blurted out anxiously.

She spoke softly, carefully, and kindly and asked if she could hold my hand. I started to panic even more. She pulled up a chair next to me and paused for what seemed like an eternity. "My name is Kia, and I am here to answer as many questions as I can for you about last night. Why don't you lie back and take a few deep breaths. I know this is confusing. Your mom is outside in the waiting room. You will get to see her soon, but I think it is best if we talk for a bit first."

I did not want to calm down or take a damn breath. I wanted to know what the hell was going on. I thought about running out of that room, half naked under my hospital gown. But more than anything, I wanted answers, even if those answers would bring me to my knees. "Okay, can you please tell me what is going on?" I was trying to stay as calm as I could.

Kia held my hand beside me. Squeezing softly, she carefully spoke the words that changed my life forever. "Sky, we think you may have been sexually assaulted last night."

I started sobbing inconsolably. I tried to get up from the squeaky hospital bed, unsure of what I was doing next, but I knew I did not want to hear another word. What Kia said next was a blur, but somehow, she got me back in bed and calmed me down. I took huge gulps of water as heavy tears rolled down my face. "What do you mean? Sexually assaulted? But how?" I was trying to put the pieces of the night prior back together in my head.

She was soothing amid the heaviness and chaos of the moment. Even though I did not know her, I could gather that she was there to help me. She let me cry as long as needed and ask any questions I had.

She explained that the night prior, the police received a call to an abandoned house I was at, and they found me in a walk-in closet with my clothes off. They had brought me to the hospital and had monitored me for the rest of the night until I finally woke up. I was in pure disbelief. How had this happened? I tried to piece the night before back together, but my headache was vicious, and I could not think straight to save my life.

Kia, who I later came to find out was a sexual abuse counselor, told me to take all the time I needed. But I could tell she was waiting on me to fill in some of the blanks of the night before. "There is no rush, Sky. We will talk at your pace when you are ready. Can you start telling me what you remember from last night?" she said as gently as she could.

At this point I had known this woman for all of maybe twenty minutes, and I had to walk her through one of, if not *the,* worst nights of my life. I took a giant deep breath and closed my eyes, hoping to recollect all the details of what had happened. It all came rushing back and landed on me like a shit ton of bricks. Like a rewind button in a movie, my mind went straight back to where it all started the day before.

The day before was Friday, a school day. As a junior in high school I was sixteen. My two friends and I had made a plan to meet up with these guys we had met at a Halloween party a few months prior. These guys lived in a city about twenty minutes away. The plan was that after school we would get on public transportation and meet them for a night of *fun.* We only spent a few hours with this group months before, so we had no idea where they would take us, what we would be doing, or if they were safe or not. But at that time, we were uninhibited in every way. We just wanted to have a good time, and we were definitely not thinking of any consequences that could come of it. When you are a teenager, you think you are invincible, or at least that is how I felt.

When they picked us up it was not the group I had anticipated. Two of the guys I recognized, but one guy I had never seen before. I guess one of the guys from Halloween night could not make it, so they decided to bring another friend along. We got in their yellow Hummer without question and immediately drove to a store we knew sold liquor without checking IDs. The girls and I picked out a 750 ml bottle of E&J Brandy and got back in the car, anxious for where the night would take us.

"Where to?" I asked.

The energy in the car was palpable. I could sense this nervous but exciting rush as we anticipated our next move. Us girls were giddy but trying to play it cool. We had been planning this night for weeks, so we knew we would make it a night to remember.

We drove around for a while until we stopped at a park to smoke some weed. My friends were not smokers, so they did not partake, but I did not want to be a party pooper. I took several hits. Heaviness in my limbs and haziness in my mind followed.

"Let's head to the next spot," one of the guys, named Mike said, motioning to the car. We all hopped in, ready for the next destination.

They would not tell us where we were driving next. "It's a surprise. Don't worry. It's a cool spot," Mike said assuringly.

Looking back, this was one of many red flags that night. Especially since I did not really know or trust any of these guys. But again, I did not want to rain on our parade, so I just smiled and went along.

We finally drove up to a huge tract home in a residential neighborhood. The area was quiet and lit only by streetlights. Most of the houses on the street had their lights off. It felt eerie and unsettling. I wondered if one of the guys lived here.

"Whose house is this?" my friend Mary asked.

There were no signs of people living in the house we pulled up to. No cars in the driveway, no porch or inside lights on. We got out of the obnoxiously bright yellow Hummer, and they took us through the backyard and to an unlocked window. *Are we going to get in trouble for this?* I thought. But everyone seemed sure about it, so one by one, we climbed into a room in this dark abandoned house.

We all wandered around this huge, dark house but eventually gathered in a small room on the first floor. We opened up the bottle of E&J and passed it around, but my friends and I were the only ones taking swigs. I definitely drank the most out of everyone, and I knew I was getting drunk. But I wanted to keep the fun going, so I kept drinking.

Hours went by. I remember us laughing a lot, listening to music, and having a great time. The one guy I did not know beforehand was trying to get close and talk to me. My two friends were paired up with the other two guys, so I think he assumed he and I would eventually pair up. I had made it very clear, though, in front of the group, that I was *not* interested. I remember at one point saying I had a boyfriend just to send him the message.

The last memory I have from that night is of the six of us sitting down on the carpet inside that small room, laughing and talking. That was it. It all goes blank after that. I found out what happened in full the next morning, trying to piece everything and anything back together. But I could not recollect a thing between my last memory and waking up in the hospital. One moment I was drinking out of the bottle of E&J and having fun with my friends, and the next moment I was in a hospital bed, panicked, scared, and hungover. And just like that, my life would change forever.

Once I had calmed down, I told the counselor, Kia, everything I could remember. It took me a while to explain it all. I kept stopping and trying to fill in the blanks.

She then explained what the police had told her and what my friends had told the police. "Your friends and two of the guys went to other parts of the house at one point in the night. You stayed downstairs with a guy whose name was Gabe. They said that when they left, you were conscious, or they thought you were. Sometime later, a neighbor called the police. They heard noises coming from the house and thought it was suspicious since they knew no one lived there. When the police arrived and entered the home, they found you alone in a closet on the house's first floor, passed out, and without your clothes on."

Kia explained everything the police had relayed to her. She handed me tissues as tears rolled down my cheeks for what seemed like forever. Having a stranger recall horrible details of what happened to you, that you have no recollection of, is terrifying beyond belief.

After running through all the details from the night before with Kia, a doctor came in and asked to speak with me. At that moment, I had just received the scariest and heaviest information at what seemed like a mile a minute. I could not wrap my head around it. They asked for my consent to perform the rape kit, and I agreed. I needed to know what happened for sure. Uncomfortable and horrified, I prayed none of it was true.

Once they finished the test, I could finally see my mom. That moment etched itself into my mind forever. Seeing the grief, pain, and fear in her eyes shook me and still shakes me to my very core. I thought of what she must have been going through, seeing me this way and knowing what most likely happened to me. She stood there quietly, which was not the norm for her. I could tell she wanted to take me into her arms and ask me a million questions, but she tried her best to keep her composure.

Just as scared, I sat there silently, not knowing how to act around her. It may sound crazy, but I had more fear for her to know someone sexually assaulted me than for me to hear that confirmed. I could handle it, and I could process it alone.

But for her to know and for her heart to shatter in the way I knew it would, completely deflated me.

Hours passed, and the doctor finally entered the room where my mom, Kia, and I were waiting. He explained the rape kit had confirmed I *had* been sexually assaulted the night before. I sat in bed, still and unmovable. I did not react, cry, or say anything. I could not believe this reality.

After a full day in the hospital, they finally released me. During the car ride home, I had to have my mom stop the car twice so I could throw up on the side of the road. It shook me in every sense of the word. When we made it home, my dad hugged me while I cried on his shoulder. I wanted to be anywhere but in my own skin. I was scared to see the same look on his face that my mom had when I first saw her. My mind raced, not only from what I experienced but from what my poor parents were going through.

Can they ever look at me the same again? Are they blaming themselves? Are they blaming me? A flood of questions permeated my mind. My mom suggested I take a nap, but I was afraid I'd fall asleep and have to remember everything that had happened all over again once I woke up. I was living out my worst nightmare without any escape.

That weekend, the police stopped by my house and filed a police report with all the details I could remember from that night. He explained they would pursue the case, and they would charge Gabe. I personally wanted this all to go away. I wanted to put it behind me and never speak of it again. But what followed was a series of court dates, meetings with my public defender, and ultimately the moment I had to speak in front of the court. I had to explain in detail everything that happened that night while his lawyer interrogated me.

His lawyer made sure to paint a picture that put me at fault. His lawyer was a woman. *How can you defend this person? What if I was your daughter? Would you still be making me out to be a drunk slut who asked for this?* The hardest thing I had to do that day was to look *him* straight in the face and tell my story without crumbling. I held my head high and tried to speak as clearly as possible. I knew I had to do this, and I could not shy away from speaking the truth.

His sentence included probation and a year at a boys' camp somewhere far away. I felt relief I could *finally* put this behind me and start to put the pieces back together to move forward. The state required I see a therapist. Her name was Dianne, an older woman with a warm disposition. I could tell she had heard many stories like mine. She was comforting and supported me during one of the most difficult times in my life. She helped me process what had happened for the following year. During that time, I was able to start healing and get to a better place with this new reality. Still, a voice lived in my head, taking the blame for what happened that evening.

I could have avoided this. I should not have drunk that much. I should not have agreed to hang out with guys I did not even know well. I should have never gone into that abandoned house. I should not have drunk. I should not have drunk. I should not have drunk. Those thoughts dominated my mind for years to come. I continued attending therapy and talked through it with my incredibly supportive parents and friends.

I did not hold it in. Yet those thoughts still lingered in my head, no matter what I did. In full disclosure, those thoughts still come up almost fifteen years later.

It has been a very long time since that all happened. I have healed. I have processed and formed a lot of acceptance around the situation since. I have continued to see other therapists, and I have unpacked this traumatic event over and over. I have worked hard over the years to let go of the blame I placed on myself. But truthfully, I cannot say I have fully let that blame go or the deep-seated belief that I did have some fault in what happened.

Ultimately, I did make decisions that evening that led to passing out and full vulnerability. But I have accepted and acknowledged that no matter what state I was in, no one had the right to violate me or take advantage of me in the way he did. I was not in a place to give proper consent in a fully unconscious state. And what he did was his choice. He made a decision and violated me. That was *not* my fault, nor will it ever be. I have had to work hard to get to this place of acceptance and to let a lot of the blame I placed on myself go. And I finally feel free from it. It no longer has a hold on me like it once did.

For a while, after this happened, I decided not to drink, go to parties, or go out in general. I focused on finishing high school and took a more cautious approach to life. I was still healing and trying to figure out how to truly deal with what had happened. I was still learning how to be in social situations without being anxious. Thankfully, I always had great friends around me to support me.

After some time, I did start to go out to social events, and eventually, I started drinking again. I have to say that when I started drinking again, I did feel guilty and judged. *How can I drink again after something like that happened to me while under the influence?* That was something I thought about a lot, but I wanted to get back to my life and feel like I was the same me, maybe with more precautions, but still me nonetheless.

I started to let my guard down more, and I started living with less fear. In the years to come, I can say that I put myself in situations where I was really drunk again, and I made myself vulnerable. As I sit here and reflect on that now, it makes me cringe.

Part of me wishes I had stopped drinking after that traumatic event and learned the lesson of never placing myself in a vulnerable situation again. But that isn't my truth. The truth is, I sometimes allowed myself to become inebriated, and thus, experienced other traumatic events, such a losing my front two teeth because of a fight at a club. That did happen, and many may say I did not learn my lesson. I do not necessarily agree with that because today, at thirty years old, I do believe I have. It is just not the linear path I hoped for or expected to take.

Healing, learning, processing, and understanding are not always linear journeys. Most of us repeatedly fall before we learn our lessons. And learning our lessons can take twists and turns and years to really learn. In my humble opinion, what matters is that we keep picking ourselves up and keep fighting. What matters is the lessons we take away from what we have gone through.

If I could go back to tell my younger self anything, it would be to protect myself, not to trust everyone, not even myself at times. I would remind myself to move with caution because horrible things can happen, even when it seems like we are invincible. Those are some of the same things I still tell myself, especially when I am out and making a choice to drink.

This situation has not been easy for me to talk about with many people, even some of the closest people in my life. As I mentioned, I was apprehensive about sharing it with the world while writing this book. If I am honest, for a long time, I believed the minute people found out about this, it would place a mark on me. I thought people would pity me, misunderstand me, or look at me differently. I have finally gotten to a place where it does not bother me if somebody does.

I once read a quote,

"You can't fully love yourself and hate your experiences" (Dykstra 2018).

That hit me like a ton of bricks because in the lifelong journey of truly loving myself, I have hated some of the things I have been through. I have carried a lot of shame surrounding them. But, after significant self-work, I have realized everything I have been through surrounding alcohol, and as a whole, has crafted and evolved me into the woman I am today. All the good and all the bad.

One experience does not define me. But I am who I am because of what I have learned through each and every experience I have lived through. I have decided to no longer live in shame or be afraid to be who I am and to show who I have *been*.

The road, windy and turbulent as it has sometimes been, has ultimately led to where I stand today—a fully formed, evolved work in progress. I hope you can continue reading my story with an open heart and mind. And if you take anything away from it, I hope you let go of any of the shame you carry from what you have gone through. It is where we are today that counts, and we are stronger for it.

CHAPTER 3:

A Club Fight

It wasn't until we got in line for the club that I started to get nervous about my cousin's ID passing the check. My hands started to sweat, and I could feel myself getting hot. I tried not to look suspicious and remembered the details on my cousin's ID. I took a few deep breaths and kept telling myself it would work. I just had to try.

It was my best friend Arianna's twenty-first birthday, and I could not miss this epic celebration. We had been thinking about this night for months. We could not wait to go out and finally get into a club legally. Well, not me; I was still nineteen. But at least Arianna could, and I had my older cousin's ID. Except, my cousin looked absolutely nothing like me.

My cousin's skin is about seven shades darker than mine, she is way taller and thinner than I am, and she has completely different facial features. But I had the ID in my wallet anyway, praying it would get me into Infusion Lounge—this popular and happening club in downtown San Francisco.

It was a Saturday, and I worked at Nordstrom at the time. That day, I had worked a full nine-hour shift, gotten changed into the tightest dress I could find, and met my best friend and our group for what we hoped would be a fun night on the town.

When I got to the bouncer, I handed my (cousin's) ID to him as smoothly as possible and tried not to look at him too intently. He scanned the ID, staring at it for longer than I would have liked, but he let me in. Score! One step closer to a fabulous night.

We immediately started drinking. Our drink of choice— Adios Motherfuckers. If you have never had one before, don't. It is a drink I have gladly vowed never to touch again. You make an Adios with vodka, rum, tequila, gin, *and* blue curaçao, a recipe for disaster with a vicious hangover. We started pounding them while the club filled to the brim with sweaty, drunk, and sloppy people. I, unfortunately, was on my way to becoming one of them.

A few more friends joined us, and it started to really become a *party*. We were dancing, drinking our Adioses like it was our jobs, and having the time of our lives. It was one of those nights that felt like nothing could go wrong and that we wanted to last forever—until everything changed.

As the night got later, more and more people started piling into this already small club. It became overly crowded, with basically no room for any personal space. Walking to the bathroom was an ordeal because of the sea of people we had to go through. At one point, I noticed a group of girls show up. And even though I was already quite tipsy, they were loud and seemed very drunk. I assumed they were there for their own celebration because they had a decorated VIP table to themselves.

For some reason, our group kept ending up near their table. This group of girls were older than us, maybe mid-twenties. Dressed to the nines, endless bottles of champagne appeared in their section. I gathered they had money, or at least their dates did. They were obnoxious and unaware of their surroundings, as they kept bumping into us and spilling drinks near us. I tried to ignore it and continue having a good time with my friends, but I was getting increasingly annoyed. I also noticed myself getting progressively drunker as the minutes went by, which was not a good combination in a small, loud, and packed nightclub as an underaged person.

A few drinks spilled around us, which I could get over. But at one point, they spilled some alcohol all over my friend's shoes. I had to say something. Yes, the club was packed, and it was easy to bump into one another and maybe even spill some, but this seemed excessive. I wanted it to stop, so I could get back to having fun.

I tapped the girl who had spilled on my friend's shoes. "Can you please chill out and stop spilling everywhere? You just spilled on my friend, and it is getting everywhere. Seriously, chill."

She nodded dismissively and acted like she did not hear me. She then continued talking with her friends.

I could tell they were saying things about me because they kept looking over where I was. Looking back, it all sounds so stupid and juvenile, but at the time, it pissed me off. I decided to let it go and get back to my friends. I was not going to let them ruin our night, or so I thought.

My friends and I kept making our way back to the bar to order more Adios cocktails. I stood at the bar beside a friend from junior college I'd invited, Jessica. I realized we had lost the rest of our group in the crowd. We inched our way to the bathroom, to another dance floor, and back to the bar, but there was still no sign of our group. After looking for them all over the club, we decided to stay put. We figured we would find them at some point. But then, Jessica ended up running into a friend in the VIP section and motioned for us to come over.

We walked over, and she invited us into her section. My feet were killing me, so I was thrilled to find a place to sit and relax for a bit. The VIP section was tiny. Basically, a few tables, a ton of champagne and other alcohol bottles, and a ton of people standing around. Now we were even closer to those obnoxious girls that kept spilling drinks.

I sent my best friend a text, asking where she and the rest of our group was. No response. I had not found a place to sit yet, so I walked over to a corner with an empty chair and sat down. I took my shoes off and tried gathering my bearings. I was dizzy, exhausted, and very drunk.

It took me a few minutes to realize where I had flopped down to sit was at the edge of the table where these stupid, drunk girls were seated. The next thing I knew, they were hovering over me as we exchanged blurry curse words at each other. It got louder and more aggressive, so I ended up standing up as the girls screamed in my face. At that moment, it dawned on me I was alone. My friend, Jessica, was not around me anymore.

I looked around, trying to scan for her, and could not see her. Now I found myself knee-deep in a screaming match with three drunk girls while drunk myself—another recipe for disaster. We contained it to words and yelling until one of the girls lunged forward at me. That is when I grabbed her and pushed her back with as much force as possible, and she fell on top of one of her friends. I was shocked.

I did not mean to make her fall. I just needed to get her out of my face before she dropped me first. Once the other people in their group realized what was happening and that their friend had fallen, a guy with dark hair bum rushed me and decided he would tell me off. I had not even noticed this guy before, and to be completely honest, I thought he was all talk—my mistake. We talked shit to each other that seemed like gibberish until he crossed the line in a way I genuinely did not expect.

He touched around the table next to him like he was looking for something while he kept his eyes on me. I had no clue what this guy was looking for on the table until, in one swift motion, he grabbed an empty Grey Goose bottle from an ice bucket on a table next to us and struck me with it directly across the face. It happened all at once but also in slow motion. I ended up laid out on the ground, but with adrenaline running as high as it could, I got up back up as quickly as I could.

I grabbed a bottle from that same ice bucket and threw it toward them when suddenly, a huge bouncer picked me up and pulled me into a corner. It was not until the bouncer got me into the corner that I finally came back into my body and realized what had just happened. I wiped my face and tasted something like metal. Blood was coming from my mouth, and that is when I felt it. He'd cracked my two front teeth in *fucking half.*

I started screaming hysterically and trying to explain to the bouncer what the guy had done. From the way the bouncer had grabbed me initially, I did not think he had seen what the guy had done to provoke me. "That guy hit me in the fucking face with that bottle," I screamed at him.

He tried to calm me down to no avail. And as luck would have it, I guess the only thing the bouncers had seen was me throwing a bottle at that group and not that man striking me in the face with the bottle first. *Where the hell are my friends? What am I going to tell my parents? What am I going to do about my teeth? What the fuck?* I collapsed to the floor.

The bouncers took me to a back-office area that was quiet and cold. They asked me for my name and to see my ID. *Oh shit.* While they hadn't cared about my cousin's ID before, now that they thought I had started a fight in their VIP section, I was sure they would. This was bad. I told them I thought I had lost my ID, and I fake scrambled in my purse. I looked up with what I knew was a pitiful look on my face. "Look, I am just nineteen."

The club did not call the police because the establishment would have gotten into trouble for having an obviously drunk underage girl who just got into a fight with now two broken front teeth. "This is your lucky day," they told me because I would otherwise have been in trouble.

"Look at my teeth! Look at my damn teeth. He hit me in the face with a bottle. Are you serious? Do you know who this guy is?"

They wouldn't answer my questions, and it was clear they wanted me to get the hell out of their club. You would think seeing me with two shattered front teeth would induce a little compassion, but these bouncers were cold and aloof. They dismissed what I said and acted extremely bothered.

Thankfully, my friends *finally* came rushing in. I had asked one of the friendlier bouncers to please find them and tell them what had happened. My friends started freaking out when they saw me. Amid the absolute chaos, my best friend started crying. The bouncers had enough of us for the evening and escorted us out of the club. My friends, like me, were trying their best to get answers as to who did this. But the bouncers ignored our questions and gave us nothing.

We left hysterical and in shambles. I remember trying to piece together what happened on the car ride home, recalling each detail, and trying to make sense of it. I tried to remember the details of his face. I kept licking over my broken front teeth as salty tears streamed down my face. *Did that really happen?* My mind was having trouble catching up to reality.

That night, I slept over at my best friend's house because I couldn't face my parents yet. I had had enough emotion for the night. All I wanted to do was go to sleep and wake up with unscathed teeth.

The next day, I woke up, and for a few moments, I did not remember what had occurred. I propped myself out of my best friend's bed, only to look in the mirror hanging on her wall. Instantly, it came rushing back. My face was swollen and sore. I was ridiculously hungover and exhausted. Oh, and I had two cracked front teeth. *Is this real?*

My parents picked me up, and I had to give them a detailed version of what had happened. Because I had been so drunk the night before and a lot of what happened was fuzzy in my head, explaining was difficult. That made me feel extremely pathetic. I was also still a little drunk, so I tried to explain while holding back from throwing up.

I pretty much blacked out on how my parents reacted. It was all too much. Once I described how my face got so fucked up, they drove me to the hospital. Because of the impact of the bottle on my face, they wanted to make sure I was okay.

We spent most of the day at the urgent care. That day was like living in an out-of-body experience—watching myself talk to doctors, open my cut-up mouth, and having to retell the events that happened.

A few days after that horrific night, my parents followed up with the club to see if they identified the guy who struck me. As it turned out, they said they did not have cameras placed where the incident happened, so they couldn't identify the guy based on my description. It seemed like a lost cause, but I didn't care about that. It might have been good to know who the man was that struck me across the face. And maybe I would have been vindicated in some way if he had been held accountable. But what I really cared about was that, once again, I had experienced a traumatic event while drunk.

I had thought I had it all under control. Even though I had been underaged at a club, drunk, and had lost my friends in the crowd, I still never thought the night could take such a vicious turn. That was a problem, and I knew it. I still had not learned my lesson with playing with fire—in my case, in the form of alcohol.

At age thirty, more than a decade later, this incident has impacted my life and continues to shape the way I maneuver through the world. I used to be quite fearless when I was younger, throwing caution to the wind often. I thought I was strong and smart, and even though I had already been through tough experiences, it did not stop me from putting myself in harm's way. I had once again vowed, like many times in the past, not to drink again.

As for my physical scars, thankfully, my mother had worked in the dental field years prior, so one of her dentist friends was able to fix my teeth. I remember being incredibly embarrassed when I sat in the dental chair, and he asked me how it had happened. He repeatedly reminded me how fortunate

I was that the nerves in my front two teeth didn't sever. I stopped going out for a while after that. I even stopped drinking for a while. I was still under twenty-one, after all. Though it shook me up, I still had not fully grasped the correlation between my drinking and the trauma often ensued in my life.

That night ended up being one to remember, just not how we initially thought it would be. It's a night I still think about with pain and embarrassment. I realized the moment I decided to drink that night I had relinquished a level of control. *Anything* can happen when you inebriate yourself and are not in control of all your senses. A lot of us do not always think about consuming alcohol that way.

That does not mean something bad is always bound to happen, but the possibility of it significantly increases when drinking. Especially when you are out in public, around people you do not know. That man should have never smashed a bottle across my face. But maybe it would not have happened had I been sober enough to remove myself from the situation before it escalated.

This was another wake-up call for me at a young age. I would continue to have many more. This particular one came in the form of two broken front teeth and emotional scars that have not faded easily, even after a long time.

Now, after many years have passed, I still get nervous when I am out. Even if I have only had one or a few drinks, I always know things can turn for the worst in a matter of seconds. I am stronger, smarter, and wiser now, but that does not make me feel invincible. None of us are. *Anything can happen, especially in the company of alcohol.*

I enjoy going to a nice bar with friends occasionally, but I will never forget what happened. I always hear a little voice in my head saying, *Anything can happen.*

CHAPTER 4:

Spiral

When I was in my early twenties, I felt lost without a compass. My boyfriend and I were on a loop of on again off again for a few years. It was a classic young twenties love story, consuming, intoxicating, and confusing all in one. Even though we were best friends and had love between us, we were young and inexperienced. The highs were high, and the lows were low, leading to instability. This rocked my world and left me on my knees repeatedly. I started using alcohol in a way that I hadn't before and drinking more than I ever had in the past.

From the time I began drinking at the age of fifteen, I was doing it out of curiosity, fun, and because I thought it was the cool thing to do around my friends. Those reasons were my driving force behind continuing to pick up booze for a while. But things shifted for me in my early twenties. I started consuming alcohol, as I would later understand, as a crutch and a vice. I definitely did not fully understand the gravity of this at the time, but I spent years using it as a comfort blanket, one that would bring me the exact opposite of that.

Because I was young and inexperienced, I did not know how to even begin processing heartbreak. I was experiencing things I had never before, and I wanted so badly to run away from that, no matter what it would take. I do not think anyone likes to go through emotional pain, but I would say at this time in my life, facing my pain was something I would do anything to avoid. I did not know how to work through a breakup or how to cope with any of the new emotions permeating my life at this time.

I was in a truly dark place. The kind of darkness that is all-consuming and makes you believe it will suffocate you. I did not want to ask for help from my parents or my friends. Overwhelmed and unequipped, I turned to an old friend I believed could make it go away, at least for a while. Since I had already been drinking for several years at this point, overdrinking was nothing new to me. However, a drunk night beforehand would be full of fun with friends. Not anymore.

I drank every day after work, all day on weekends, and whenever I would start not being able to withstand the emotions caused by my breakup. Some days I walked to the liquor store during my lunch break and drank until I had to clock back in. My life spiraled completely out of control.

I jumped from job to job. I spent weekend after weekend at friends' houses, avoiding going home. I ran away from my life and my feelings all together. I became a walking zombie, doing everything I could to be anywhere but in my skin and my body. I was reckless, devastated, avoidant, and terrified. I wanted anything but to confront the issues piled up beside me. Alcohol had become the easy escape from this rollercoaster I was on. I did not realize how it would dramatically affect my family, friends, and me over the course of a few years.

I lived at my parents' house during this turbulent time, which was quite difficult. I have always been a private person who likes to isolate myself when I am not doing well. Some find comfort around people they love. I have always been the very opposite. I like to figure out my shit alone and emerge only once healed and better. So my family seeing me so broken was like someone exposing me and being on display at my very worst.

I felt like the worst version of myself, falling apart right in front of them. Even being around my family and sitting at the dinner table was challenging. I knew I had become a shell of myself and was afraid of what they saw when they looked at me. It is important to note that historically I had always kept a close relationship with my parents, so this period affected us greatly.

I am an only child, and our family of three has been close-knit as long as I have been alive. I knew they could see something seriously off with me. Regardless of how much I avoided speaking about it or opening up. They knew. They saw I had been crying night after night, barely sleeping, and drinking like it was my job. Even so, I could not bring myself to seek their help and open up about what I went through. I wanted so desperately to be away from my home and my family, so they would not have to see me in a state where I could barely stand myself. It may seem crazy, but even though I knew how dire things were getting, I could not stop self-sabotaging.

As badly as I wanted to get away from my family, I now know I needed them most at that time. Running away from them and my problems only dug myself deeper into a series of more pain and loss of control in my life. I spent weeks on end at my best friend's house. I barely checked in with my family, so they rarely knew where I was. They would call and text me, asking where I was or what I was doing. I would either not respond or deflect. I avoided everything and everyone I could.

I knew I could spend time at my best friend's place because he knew what I was going through. Most importantly, he knew how to leave me alone. But left to my own devices, I went down a rabbit hole and fast. I called off from work repeatedly, drank all day, and slept to escape my reality. I did everything to run away from confronting all the emotions that were hurting me so badly.

One day, like many others, I stayed at my best friend's house. He had been at work, and I walked myself to the corner store and bought a forty. That was pretty much the only thing I could afford because I was also not budgeting my money well those days. I walked home and cracked the forty open on a Tuesday at around 1:00 p.m. That moment stood out to me, even within the daze I found myself in.

How did I let myself get here? I was worried my best friend would see the empty forty bottle when he got home a few hours later, so I walked it to his neighbor's trash bin. I had hit a new low that day. The heartbreak I carried was heavier than ever, and my alcohol problem dawned on me.

This could have been the point in the story where I turned things around and pumped the brakes on my drinking, but I didn't. I leaned into it, and my life became more out of control. My parents lived in fear of where I was, who I was with, and where I would end up. I went radio silent on them and myself. I could not bear an honest look in the mirror, so I didn't. I kept sabotaging myself and did what I knew best at that time—avoid, avoid, avoid at all costs.

I had lost my first adult job out of college because I had called out one too many times. I saw this coming because they warned me repeatedly, but I did not care. I did not care much for myself or my life. I lived moment to moment, pretending like I had an ounce of my life together. Even from the outside looking in, it was clear I was losing it.

I had decided to go back home at one point once I had been let go of my job. This meant I was drinking all day at home instead of at my best friend's house. On one gloomy Thursday morning, I already had a few glasses of wine in me by 11:00 a.m. My parents had left for work, so I was at home getting drunk to pass the time and numb my emotions. I called my best friend, who I must have worried because after talking to me for about twenty minutes, he reached out to my dad at work. He told my dad I was home drinking myself into oblivion and I shouldn't be alone.

I knew things were bad, but I could not understand the level of concern and worry I caused everyone around me. I have hit several rock bottoms in the course of my life, but this day was a marker for me. I knew I had been spiraling out of control for a while, but the gravity of it finally hit me hard.

Any other time, I would have been angry with my best friend for calling my parents and telling them anything I hadn't told them myself. But this time, I not only understood, but I was almost happy he did so. I had been off the rails. During this particular week, I had been drinking from the time I woke up until I passed out. It seemed like the darkest hours of my life. It was almost like I was crying for help silently in my room, wishing someone would force me out of this mess.

My dad came home around 1:00 p.m. and found me in my room, crying, hungover, and a little drunk. He scooped me into his car and drove me to Mental Health at Kaiser. When we got to the packed waiting room, the staff told us it would be a while. We sat there in silence, waiting for them to call my name. I knew I looked like such a mess sitting there in that waiting room. I had not slept much, wine stained my lips red, and I appeared dressed like a slob.

When they called me back, I spoke to a very cold and abrupt woman. After answering some of her routine questions, she informed me they would not be able to further assist me that day because I had drunk in the last twenty-four hours. I guess that is one of their protocols. She told me I could come back and see someone once I was fully sober. This was when I needed the help most. But I needed to come back once I was sober? That did not make a lick of sense to me at the moment. I could tell from the way she looked at me she could see how shattered I was. Not in an empathetic way, but with a look of disgust.

My dad drove us home, and I cried the entire way. I was ashamed; something I would come to often associate with alcohol. *When did alcohol start being this dark hole that sucked me in and stopped being fun?*

I realized the quicksand alcohol had become for me, especially when I felt my lowest. What I thought would numb my hurt had become something that brought me even more pain and disaster. This left me more isolated, scared, and in more angst than I had started with.

When I looked in the mirror, it was clear to me that alcohol was not fun anymore. It had become this vice that kept me down and effected pretty much every area of my life. It was dark, hollow, and I felt trapped. But finally, I knew I had to get off the ride. It was time to stop running away and avoiding my emotions. I needed help, and I had to be willing to receive it. I had let things spiral for far too long, and I knew it would only worsen if I did not seek the assistance that I so desperately needed.

In the following months, I leaned heavily on my family and close friends. I forced myself to be vulnerable and open, and I stopped avoiding showing up as I actually was. I stopped pretending I was okay and worked on healing, one day at a time. I accepted the things I could not change. My breakup was one of them. And I began working on changing the things in my control—daily movement, nutrition, and mental health. I found a new therapist named Evelyn—an older woman who did not handle me with kid gloves. She was straightforward and asked me eye-opening questions that sparked change within me. For the first time in a while, I had a game plan for moving forward that was healthy, manageable, and sustainable.

I worked with my therapist for a year and a half. It was incredibly challenging confronting my inner demons and working through some of the pain I was still holding on to, but it felt good to do right by myself. My issues and my dependency with alcohol at that time did not go away overnight, and I was not suddenly cured. I still had moments when I was stressed and anxious, and alcohol seemed like the answer. But I knew with all my being going back to where I was a few months ago—drinking all day, sad in a dark room—was no longer an option.

I could see how therapy, being honest with myself, and being open with my loved ones were truly helping me. My life had become increasingly stable, and I could sense peace within my being again. I had tough days, and on those days, instead of numbing it, I acknowledged the pain. I sat with it and worked through it with the new tools I had learned.

If I took one thing away from this dark period in my life, it is that you can only run from your pain or discomfort for so long before it catches up to you. And once it does, it will all come crashing down in ways you would not even imagine. The more running you do, the more the disaster piles up. I had learned that alcohol could be my worst enemy when I used it to escape being uncomfortable, whether that be stress, pain, worry, fear, or anxiety. Alcohol had brought me to my knees. And I had to do even more heavy lifting to get back up than I would have if I had just confronted my feelings head-on.

All the running and avoiding I did just caused me more pain and isolation. When faced with emotional pain or trauma, the easiest things to pick up are the vices that seemingly sooth us. It can be a hard lesson to realize that these vices do the exact opposite and end up causing tons of damage.

Thankfully, we always have the choice to break free from these vices and fight against them. I am so grateful I could work my way out of that rollercoaster and seek the help I truly needed. The work is never easy, and it is not without misstep. But it is worth it. My journey has been far from perfect, but I finally found my compass. And I will redirect it as many times as necessary, but I am not going back to where I once was.

CHAPTER 5:

Broken Commitments

———

As I approach thirty years old in a few months, one thing I have been reflecting on is how alcohol, and my specific relationship to it, has many faces. It isn't just one thing, one way all the time. It doesn't always play out in the same way, and although I have seen definite patterns, I can say I have experienced a wide range of outcomes and feelings when it comes to it. I have lived a plethora of drunken nights resulting in many painful and heavy outcomes. But believe it or not, that was not the single most important reason I decided to start working on my relationship with alcohol.

As I started paying more attention to my life and my habits surrounding alcohol, I realized my use was holding me back from becoming the woman I had always envisioned myself becoming. These drunken disastrous nights were hurting me. The *little* decisions I made around alcohol, the debilitating hangovers, and the habits I had formed while drinking kept me on a loop. I felt like a hamster on a wheel, running in place. But I kept myself on that loop for years.

I cannot tell you how many important appointments I have had to reschedule, to-do lists I have ignored, and commitments I have made with myself that I have broken because of my habits with alcohol. Looking back, I am still ashamed of how much time I have spent hungover. I have wasted entire weekends because of a bad hangover—time that I will never get back. Once I admitted that to myself, I knew I had to implement change in my relationships with alcohol if I wanted to have any chance at becoming a woman I could be proud of.

In the last few years, I have thought alcohol had less of a stronghold on me, and I was in control of this relationship because at least really bad things had stopped happening while I was drunk. I wasn't getting black-out drunk anymore. I didn't have to apologize profusely for things I said or did. I didn't have to deal with drunk messy outcomes. But for a while, I was still drinking quite a bit for most people's standards, on a more regular cadence than I was proud of.

I started noticing a pattern that affected me even more than some of the crazy shit I have been through over the course of my life due to alcohol. I no longer had to clean up or pick up the pieces of a night gone terribly wrong, but I was still spending weekends in bed, wasting what felt like a huge portion of my life. My consumption was no longer ending in chaos, but it was clearly standing between me and my goals.

I have friends who can stay out all night drinking and still function the next day. That is not me. If I drink enough, it incapacitates me the next day. And so, I spent what seemed like an endless number of weekends in bed, regretful and frustrated. But sure enough, I would do it again the following weekend. While lying around all day because of a hungover has happened to a lot of us, weekend after weekend these kinds of days piled up, and it started to feel like a real problem I couldn't get a handle on.

From the picture I have painted, it could be easy to assume I have been the type of person not to accomplish much in my life because of my relationships with alcohol. Quite the contrary, I pride myself on being a very goal-oriented and driven individual and always have been. That is why this cycle of hangovers and wasted time was such a huge issue for me and the catalyst for me to start making some real changes.

During the week, I make hour-to-hour schedules, to-do lists, and set up systems to stick to and achieve my goals. For the most part, I can stick to these commitments to get things done and inch myself closer and closer to whom I envision myself becoming—a healthy, balanced, and accomplished woman. In fact, I think I do well at making sure I am honoring the little pacts I make with myself on a daily basis, and most importantly, I feel damn good doing so. It's the one thing that makes me feel alive, like I am gifting myself every day in the form of commitment and discipline. I believe that is why I feel at my lowest and darkest on days after I have drunk a lot, and I wake up knowing nothing productive will get done that day.

In the past few years, these types of days have accumulated and created a vicious cycle. I have a solid productive week. I feel strong and confident. By the time Saturday rolls around, I feel like I can have a few drinks without any issues. The next thing you know, I am waking up on Sunday morning, only to ignore all the to-dos I have for that day, leaving me sad and angry with myself. Repeat.

Sure, some weekends don't go this way, but it has happened enough for me to say it has gotten old. I started to realize these things can and will really hold me back long term. These hangover days pile up and create a long and challenging bridge from the life of peace, accomplishment, and balance I long for. So why did I continue to let it happen time and time again?

I am still working on getting to the root of that question and understanding why I have been willing to do something that makes me feel so terrible the next day. I don't have one simple answer, but I do know it's one of many reasons why I have decided to get a real look at the role alcohol has played in my life and admit that it has been the walker and I have been the dog.

As I have tried to set boundaries for myself in the last few months, I have circled back to the saying, "Nothing changes if nothing changes." I know now I can wake up early every day to meditate, eat my greens, work incredibly hard, and end each day with a workout. But if I throw that all away on the weekends just to have a few drinks, nothing changes, and I am being extremely counterproductive. If I continue to let these types of nights control my life, they will do just that, and I won't be getting closer to this holistically centered life I want for myself. All I will be doing is running in place, changing nothing.

Mending and improving my relationship with alcohol has had many layers, and just when I feel I have fixed one thing, I start to realize another layer that needs attention. Once I got in control of my alcohol consumption enough that chaotic events were something of the past, I felt like I had somewhat gotten a hold of the negative effects of my use and that it was behind me. I thought I had a better grasp on how to control my drinking, but I didn't realize what could hurt me more was the cycle I could easily slip into. Drinking less and not throwing all caution to the wind didn't mean I wasn't ruining weekends being hungover or continuously breaking promises to myself.

I have had an almost out-of-body experience watching myself run in circles, working on becoming my best self only to throw it all away on the weekends for a night of drinks that is rarely worth it. This has impacted me in ways I am working overtime to self-correct. I am constantly working on creating and maintaining boundaries that keep me off the hamster wheel. The deeper I get into reinventing my relationship with alcohol, the more I understand this isn't a one-time fix but rather a never-ending work in progress to stop breaking commitments to myself and stop throwing my progress by the wayside for what I have been conditioned to think is a good time.

Will it ever be easy? I don't think so. That is the truth. But I believe it is a muscle I am strengthening, and I am gradually adjusting and pivoting from my old habits. Because, again, nothing changes if nothing changes.

CHAPTER 6:

Michael's Hero's Journey

I met Michael years back when we both worked for the same tech company in San Francisco. Since then, he transitioned into a wellness coach for men. I didn't know him well when we worked together, but years later, I started to see him post on LinkedIn about his struggles and the work he had done overcoming depression, idleness, and overdrinking. His candor and ability to be raw with his social media audience drew me in. It is rare to see someone show the not-so-pretty parts of being a human and expose the truths behind their growing pains. It is something I look for online, but don't often come across, so when I started seeing Michael's posts, I knew I had to connect with him in some way.

I became intrigued by Michael's story. One, because of how honest and bold he was with speaking out on his social platforms about topics like depression and alcohol that are often kept private. Second, because I had been seeking out content about people who were openly talking about their relationships with alcohol. I kept finding the same ones with the same tune—sobriety as the one and only answer. What Michael offered was different. He offered real experiences about his ongoing relationship with alcohol and how he had overcome some hardships to get to a healthy and stable place with it.

I reached out to Michael via LinkedIn and was hoping for a response, but I know life gets busy. So I was in a "hoping for the best, expecting nothing" place when I hit send. I wanted to talk with Michael about his journey with alcohol and how it got to a place where he knew something needed to change. I wanted to know how he could enact that change and, ultimately, how his life has changed because of those changes. I was pleasantly surprised when Michael agreed to hop on a call with me and discuss his relationship with alcohol and how it has evolved.

Even though Michael had agreed to speak with me, I admit I was still in shock about how open he was from the beginning of the conversation. He spoke with complete openness, which can be hard to find when discussing heavy topics like alcohol. I have found on occasions when I have brought up my own journey with alcohol people tend to get uncomfortable and even borderline judgmental. It often feels as if they are making their own silent notes about what I should and should not be discussing in public. So Michael's ability and willingness to have a raw conversation about issues that many people would rather keep behind clothes doors struck me in such a refreshing way.

Our conversation started with him explaining his relationship with alcohol a few years back when he would have up to twenty drinks with his buddies, binge eat, get terrible sleep, and then spend the next week trying to recover, just to do it all again the following Saturday. My first thought was, damn, I've been there. Like, exactly there. It's a vicious, chaotic cycle trying to rebuild your life. This can feel like a never-ending loop you cannot escape from.

"I know I was using and drinking to be the person I wanted to be. I was drinking to have fun with friends, to have the courage to go up and talk to a woman and be whatever I wanted to be," Michael explained a feeling and notion I had not thought about before. It never occurred to me people out there might be drinking to feel like someone they wished they could be. I had personally drunk for years because of stress, anxiety, and to fit in, but I had never really thought about drinking to feel like someone else. As he explained this, I immediately thought, *This is why these conversations are so important.* Everyone has a different motivating force behind why they choose what they do, and often we can be assuming and try to fill in the blanks without even knowing them. I have admittedly done this to others and have definitely had it done to me.

It seemed Michael already knew this cycle was making him unhappy, and it was something he did not want to do anymore. "I remember being out drunk on a Saturday night like I don't even want to be out here…hammered, thinking of a future day like, I can't wait for a day where I don't have to do this anymore," he said. Although this moment of acknowledgment can lead to change, a lot more than just knowing goes into creating meaningful and lasting change to end this cycle.

Michael knew there was a connection between getting shit-faced every Saturday and stuff going on inside. He understood that there was fixing to do in more areas of his life than just choosing to have one too many drinks on the weekends. He openly discussed being heavily depressed during this period and leaving the bar just to get home and cry himself to sleep many times. It was a heavy and dark time for Michael, and he knew something had to give because carrying on this way was just digging himself deeper and deeper into a hole he knew he wanted out of. This is what he called his "first level of awareness."

During this time of becoming aware that Michael's relationship with alcohol needed some adjustments, he left his career in corporate tech and began working on his own business, helping men become the healthiest versions of themselves. With this pivot came even more realizations about the weight he had been carrying in the form of depression, anxiety, and self-doubt. He was becoming aware of the root of the problems he experienced internally that affected him externally, and he understood that what needed fixing and attention was on the inside. Michael shared with me that he would often think of a future where he would not *have* to drink the way he did anymore and a space where he would maybe find a woman to spend his life with who would keep him from drinking every Saturday.

I could tell with the certainty in his voice that there was genuine belief and hope he would get through this heavy struggle.

He could envision a day when he could look at himself in the mirror and be proud of his life and who he saw staring back at him. As he started evaluating his life and choices, he saw the real effects drinking had on his mind and body.

"If I go out and get shit-faced on Saturday, maybe the hangover is only one day. But then I noticed my heart rate would remain elevated for five or six days. It would take a long time to return to baseline or other markers like HRV and sleep quality. If that's happening with the measurable stuff, what else is going on inside? I started to make the association of what I was feeling after drinking. I would get super down and depressed and unmotivated for four or five days after."

It is eye-opening and even jarring to really pay attention to the ways alcohol can affect the body and mind over time. Although acknowledging the rollercoaster alcohol can put your body through when used excessively can be scary and overwhelming, I believe it can be the catalyst of why people choose to enact change and maintain those changes. Michael had "done it long enough"—drinking weekend after weekend, letting it negatively affect his mind and body, and holding on to the self-doubt that was holding him back.

While all of us can recognize if something is holding us back, not all of us are willing to take action, and ultimately awareness does not equate to action. One thing that inspired me about Michael was not only his self-awareness throughout his journey with alcohol but his ability to take action once he knew issues were keeping him from becoming his higher self. "You can't treat the symptom," he told me, regarding the fact that many try to deal with problems with alcohol when in reality, the use or misuse of alcohol is the symptom and not the problem itself. Michael had to take a deep and honest look inward to understand the self-doubt, the depression, and the void he felt within.

"I started meditating every day to understand—what are these thought patterns? And see all of them as they are and start to dive into each of them to see where they come from. Reverse engineer them to see why they may or may not be true." He started doing the work from the inside out to heal, become more self-aware, and lean into himself. He started getting back into shape, working hard in his own business, and fueling his body and mind with nourishing food and content.

He was open to this not being a complete turnaround right away, though. "At times I would go months without it and then dip my toes back in just to realize I didn't feel good afterward." Sometimes, it can take a few rounds of trial and error, and I am glad Michael shared this because that can be the reality for most of us. He took keen notice of how he would feel after drinking and gradually realized he just enjoyed life a lot more and felt more himself without drinking regularly. He shared that not only was he taking notice of how he felt when he drank, but how he felt when he didn't drink for long periods of time. "I was waking up every day at 5:00 a.m. fired up." His body was telling him, *You're on the right track. Stay here.*

The two biggest and maybe most important questions I asked Michael were: 1) Now that you have stepped away from drinking alcohol the way you used to, do you miss it? and 2) How has your life changed as a result of it?

"The more at peace I got with myself, and happier, and realizing all the issues that I had are internal and reframing them and viewing them a different way, I have naturally seen the desire for alcohol dissipate. I don't really love how it makes me feel, during even. I never thought I would be trending to be this person who doesn't drink like I used to." Michael also noted he occasionally goes out to dinner and has a beer. The difference is now he is wildly intentional about it.

What surprised me most was his answer to my second question: "I have become a lot more in control, and being able to separate from it, and recognizing the pull and lure it has." There is so much power in realizing you are the driver of your life. You are the author of your story and the director of your own movie. Being able to exercise that power and be in more control over the things that hold you back is a gift. I initially wanted to talk to Michael because he was so candid about his struggles, and he wasn't shying away from admitting he was using alcohol in a way that was affecting him negatively. But what I didn't expect was to get a close look at the full circle that he was able to make once he took a deep look inside of himself and decided to take measurable action toward a better version of himself.

The struggles he shared with me and shares with his audiences on his social platforms are ones that many of us deal with on a daily basis. His story, like many others, can be a true source of connection, hope, and light for those feeling stuck. I see myself in a lot of his journey and found inspiration around his inner work and the intent he lives his life with now. His journey with alcohol is a testament. The work has to be done within. Only by taking action can we get to the other side of it.

CHAPTER 7:

Light in Dark Spaces

If you are wondering why I have kept my relationship with alcohol going despite it being at the epicenter of some of the scariest and terrible stories I have told you and will go on to share with you, I understand completely. It is something I, too, have asked myself over the years. So in that light, I think it is important for me to share with you some joyous times I have had while drinking and raising toasts with friends and loved ones. It isn't always bad, and it isn't always about using alcohol as a crutch or vice. I can honestly say I have had some beautiful experiences while drinking alcohol with incredible people at incredible places. Let me tell you about a few.

A BIRTHDAY CELEBRATION TO REMEMBER
For my best friend's fortieth birthday last year, all his close friends and I planned a yacht event to celebrate him for the day on the beautiful San Francisco Bay. It was the perfect day. We docked at the South San Francisco Marina, a usually very cold, windy, and often gloomy place, but not today. Today the sun shone more beautifully than ever, the breeze was perfect, and everyone looked amazing. It was one of those

moments where you know you will look back and always cherish everything about it.

His birthday came just a few months after his mother's passing of cancer. It was a complicated and heavy time for him, to say the least. This celebration had come at an incredibly timely moment for us all. We'd all had a tough year for various reasons, so we needed this event—the peace, joy, laughter, and relief. We drank delicious champagne and wine, snacked on expensive artisanal charcuterie boards, and enjoyed each other's company. I drank and cheers'd all day long and into the night. Everyone looked happy and full of life. I felt blessed to be there and in the presence of such beautiful energy. Even though this was an occasion where I had several drinks, I didn't wake up the next morning feeling regret and angst. I count it as a memory that will last a lifetime and one I can reflect on with gratitude. I know the safe, loving, and fun environment had much to do with that.

The next day, I found myself wondering if it would have been as much fun if I hadn't been drinking. Would it have been just as amazing? I think the answer is yes, but I have often thought about how we are so used to raising a toast for any celebration. I often wonder how much we rely on it to have a good time. That's when I realized two things could both be true. Maybe we do rely on drinking for any and every celebration, but maybe we create good times from the people there and the energy in the room. Not everything has to be definitive in its meaning. All I know for sure is my best friend's fortieth birthday was a beautiful day. I will always remember it with good feeling, so a toast to that!

A WEEKEND TO REMEMBER

As I have gotten older, I am happy to say my relationship with my parents has vastly improved. I am grateful we have come such a long way together and are now more like lifelong best friends. We enjoy a few glasses of good wine when we get together. They always have the greatest wine, the kind I can't afford. I have been living in Los Angeles for almost five years, almost four hundred miles from home in the Bay Area. So when I come home to visit, it is always a good time, a celebration, if you will.

A few months ago, I returned for a few days for a mother-and-daughter getaway to Calistoga, a small city in Napa Valley where they have hot springs, good wine, and the cutest bed-and-breakfast spots. I had not taken a trip with my mom or had one-on-one time with her in a while, so it was something we both looked forward to. I knew we could both use some time to chat, relax, and enjoy each other's company with no other distractions.

First stop on the trip, this beautiful winery my mom has a membership with. We had scheduled a wine tasting on their gorgeous patio overlooking the vineyard. We sat outside, sipped on some delicious wine, and caught up. In this moment, I was not drinking to take the edge off, numb any feelings, or have more fun. I just sipped on some exquisite wine, feeling fancy and enjoying the space and time with my mom. I remember studying this moment while we sat there. Not feeling the need to grab or ask for another glass but savoring the moment just as it was. Admittedly, this has not always been the case for me. I am guilty of wanting a moment never to end and feeling like drinking more will make the moment more fun. Not this day.

We went on to have dinner at one of our favorite restaurants in the area and then checked in at a picturesque boutique hotel to wrap up a perfect day. We had some wine while soaking in the hot springs at the hotel and had some really great conversations, the kind only an adult daughter and mother can have. We talked about work, our family, and our futures. Again, I started to study the moment. I did not feel the need to over drink. I did not feel the need to stay up and prolong the evening. It was perfect just as it was.

I remember getting into bed that night feeling so content, at peace, and grateful for a weekend with my mom that I will always hold close. I also felt really good. I liked being in a place where I could enjoy some wine without feeling the need to overdo it. I enjoyed savoring the moments as they were instead of trying to enhance them with another drink. The weekend could have been just as special without any wine, and maybe we will have to try that one day, but what I know is that we did sip wine, and the way that we did it felt right—not for escaping a moment, but in truly letting it be just as it is. A crutch I have used to have *more* fun, numb emotions, and escape could be used minimally, in pure peace, and just as fun. That weekend made me realize something about alcohol and my relationship with it. Light does exist in dark places.

CHAPTER 8:

KC—Like I Would Dessert

Do you remember the first event you attended after being isolated during the pandemic for two years? I wonder if it was as nerve-racking as it was for me. In March, I attended a sales kickoff conference with all my colleagues from around the country. For the first time in a long time, since the pandemic started, I found myself around a ton of people all at once. It was daunting, to say the least. I remember my boss coming up to me during the opening gala and asking me how I was doing.

"Really overwhelmed," I said with an awkward smile. "This is a lot of people. It's been a while."

Three hundred-plus people poured into a conference room at this hotel on the water in Marina del Rey. The seemingly obvious choice to loosen up was a stiff drink. *What department do you work in?* I knew it would coat each question with more ease and confidence.

As time went by, I watched as *mostly* everyone grabbed a drink and started to let their guard down to engage in informal chitchat. I walked over to the bar area to check out the options and ran into KC, this stylish girl from my team based in New York. This was my first time meeting her in person, but we'd chatted with each other over emails, Slack, and Zoom a million times. She was standing there with a clear drink with a lime in it, on the rocks—vodka soda, I thought.

"What are you drinking?" I asked.

"Just sparkling water with lime," she replied with conviction.

"Oh wow," I said before I could think of something more thoughtful to say.

The truth is, I was shocked. We were in a room full of people going for their second and third drinks for the first time in two years. I was shocked because when I had chatted with her over Zoom before, she seemed like the life of the party. If I am being honest, I think I expected her to be a girl who knocked a few back, especially at an awkward work function. But more than being surprised, I was extremely impressed. Here she was in this room with more than three hundred people that were mostly all drinking, and she chose to abstain that night.

I had a ton of questions: *Are you sober? What made you decide not to drink tonight? Is this a long-term thing?* I was drawn to her and desperately wanted to know the story behind this decision. There were better times to pick her brain, though, so I left that night with a mental note: Before this conference is over, ask KC if she would be open to sharing her journey with alcohol with me.

Dinners, happy hours, and even a sunset cruise filled the next few days, with alcohol served at each event. On each occasion, I noticed KC did not drink. She had her mocktail in hand and looked like she was having just as much fun as everyone else. As the conference went on, I grew more and more intrigued. I knew some people chose not to drink for a variety of reasons, but KC stood out to me at these events. You could tell she was not rattled by being stone-cold sober in a room full of tipsy coworkers. I wanted to know why and how she got here.

As I have mentioned, I had been searching for content and a community that discusses alcohol and its multiplicity, so I was eager to open up this dialogue with KC. I just had to pick the right time and the right approach. You never know how someone will react when asked about topics considered very private.

On the last night of the conference, I approached her at the restaurant and sat by her.

One of our coworkers yelled, "Let's take a shot, everyone!"

KC asked for water in a shot glass and *took* her shot with everyone else. She then turned to me as if she knew what I was thinking. "You know I am not completely sober, right? I drink on occasion, but I have just dramatically cut down."

Again, I was shocked. She was literally mirroring a relationship with alcohol I had been searching for on YouTube, on podcasts, in books, and within friend groups.

"How interesting," I said. "I'd love to chat more about this with you sometime."

I wanted to dive into things right then and there, but I was too shy. She seemed open and completely approachable, but even so, I knew I had to pick the right time to come straight out and ask her if she would be open to an interview about her journey to this soberish—or as she called it, damp—place.

Months went by, but I never forgot about this refreshing exchange between KC and me. Finally, one day before I could talk myself out of it, I shot her a text and asked if she would be open to hopping on Zoom to walk me through her journey with booze. She emphatically agreed, thank God. The great thing about this conversation was KC seemed at total ease diving into her relationship with alcohol. She was an open book from the start.

She started by explaining her earlier drinking habits in her mid-twenties and when she knew maybe it was time for a lifestyle adjustment. "It wasn't one thing that happened that made me rethink alcohol. Growing up in my town in Boston, everyone started drinking really young. So it got to a point where I started having anxiety or getting embarrassed, like what happened last night? That was the point where I started thinking about it."

I knew the anxiety and embarrassment she was referring to. Waking up after a night of drinking, hungover and wondering if you had said or done something wrong the night prior could be daunting and overwhelming. It could cause enough anxiety to consume the day. I would know.

She explained after going through that enough times, she started to feel like maybe going dry for periods of time would help. "I would try Dry January, and I would do it and feel good. Sometimes I'd fail. But most of the time, I was fine, and I made it through."

As someone who had done Dry January and stints of not drinking at all, I knew how empowering it could be to complete the days you had set for yourself. I have always viewed it as more of a promise and commitment you make to yourself than just abstaining from alcohol.

KC told me when her relationship with alcohol started to change. "During Covid, I started Dry November. There weren't any catalysts that sprung that month. I just said why not? It almost became a competition with myself on how long I could go. I continued on and decided I didn't need it like I thought I did."

I was truly impressed, mostly because that has not usually been my experience. In full transparency, when I have done Dry January or periods of time without drinking, I have usually been excited to enjoy a cocktail again. It sounded like KC realized alcohol did not need to occupy the same place in her life anymore. It did not seem like she had been racing to the finish line to have her next drink. I wondered what that was like.

In November 2020, KC decided to do Dry November, which propelled her to continue her journey of competing with herself to see how long she could stay committed to not drinking the way she used to. I was curious how she managed to still drink from time to time without reverting to old habits.

KC was very open about the fact she was not sober and still enjoyed having a drink on occasion when it felt worth it to her. "I still drink if it's my birthday, some special celebration, or if I'm on a trip. But it has to be worth it in my head." This was a new way of approaching alcohol from what I had been used to for most of my life. For the majority of my relationship with alcohol, I had never considered if having a cocktail was worth it. But there are so many variables to consider when deciding to drink: *Will it lead to another? Will I be hungover and ruin my day tomorrow? Will I say something I don't mean?* The list goes on.

This type of adjustment and decrease in alcohol consumption can be challenging, and I have experienced how difficult it can be to stick to the boundaries you set for yourself. Even when you know it is the thing that serves you the most, change is not easy, especially with something that is all around us all the time. I have found it is all in the small choices you make, the things you say yes and no to, and the patterns you willingly have to unlearn along the way.

KC explained small changes and adjustments made a big difference in her journey and staying committed to keeping her drinking at a minimum. "If I am going out for dinner, I'm not having wine with everyone. If everyone's getting beers at a hockey game, I am the one who is not, and I am probably the only one not drinking at the cookout, and those are the little changes that count to me because that is when it is easiest to give in."

It is jarring to think about how deeply engrained alcohol is in so much of what we do. From dinners to work events, sports games, and brunches, it is all surrounded by a glass of wine, a beer, or a fancy cocktail. So to make the decision, to repeatedly say no, when it would be much easier to say yes, is undoubtedly not an easy feat, but the kind that proves something to yourself.

It was clear to me in talking with KC that this decision to change the way she drinks and to decrease the amount of alcohol she consumes was important to her, but I wanted to know her biggest why. I have found to stick to something long term and to commit to the changes, there has to be a driving force you are investing in.

She went further into creating a competition with herself and challenging herself in that manner. "It has been a serious competition with myself, and I like feeling proud of myself. People I know have told me they have noticed me not drinking and told me they thought, *Oh, cool. You can do it. Maybe I can, too.* It also bonds people to other people in the same boat of trying to drink more intentionally and less frequently." She was not only keeping a commitment to herself but simultaneously building connections and community through this commitment.

I know it can be tough to make lifestyle changes and have the people around you not supportive of that. But when you find like-minded folks you can relate to and who encourage you on your journey, it truly can make all the difference. I asked KC how her close relationships have shifted since deciding to make adjustments to her drinking, knowing sometimes friends and family are not ready to accept these changes. Quite the opposite, KC told me her friends have not only been supportive, but some have actually made changes with alcohol themselves and have dramatically cut back. She also said it had affected the way she interacts with her friends. "I am not anxious all the time, and I can have more real sober conversations." The changes with alcohol KC had made seem to have impacted her life in such a positive way, but I personally know it's not always rainbows and sunshine.

What about the bad days? The days when you want a glass of wine to melt away the stress? Those are the times I know can be the hardest to remember your why. KC touched on this exactly and told me the hardest part could be on those rough days when you are upset or anxious, and there is nothing you can do but sit with those feelings and face them. "It does get easier because you are putting it into practice, and you learn how to face how you feel rather than run from it in a glass of red."

This moved me because I know what it is like to do both. I know what it is like to numb uncomfortable emotions with booze, and I know what it is like to sit with those emotions, stone-cold sober, and face them head-on. The only way to learn to face them is to face them repeatedly because no amount of alcohol can fix anything.

Because KC has been on this journey of decreasing her alcohol consumption drastically since the end of 2020, I wondered how she approached being in social settings during festive occasions where she chose not to drink. Peer pressure to imbibe can be difficult in social settings that would appear like the perfect time to have a drink. KC explained she likes to pick and choose what celebratory and festive occasions she drinks, and again it has to be "worth it for her." On times when she chooses not to, though, she comes with her own goodies. "If I'm going to a barbecue or I'm going to someone's house, I'll bring a case of alcohol-free seltzers. It's fun to have a prop. I'll have club soda, lime, and a rocks glass. It helps to know what you're getting. I'll even have tea if everyone's having wine because it takes the same amount of time to drink."

I love these ideas because I know it can feel out of place to have nothing in your hand when everyone else has something to sip. Although it seems small, preparation is key in these situations and going into them knowing how you will approach the situation can help navigate otherwise uncomfortable moments.

Since KC does drink on occasion, a big question I had was if the times she does drink ever make her want to drink more often? I have always thought it could be a slippery slope because if you enjoy drinking, and do it occasionally, what is to say you won't want to repeat the next weekend? KC explained it is actually the other way around a lot of the time. "What I struggle with now is if I do drink, I am like, Oh no, *what did I do?* My hangovers are ten times worse because I haven't drunk in a while and my tolerance is down, and I am always hard on myself for drinking. I am learning the balance."

We talked about the work and progress that is this new lifestyle she is living and how it is not black and white. All in all, whether you have made a change with alcohol in the past few years or the past few weeks, it is always a learning process with twists and turns. But ultimately, KC's decision to adjust her relationship with alcohol back in 2020 has served her positively in more areas of her life than one.

She mentioned she had saved so much money not going out and racking up a crazy cocktail bill. Physically, she has felt her best, and most of all, she has honored this commitment to herself over and over again.

Still, to the question of whether she could see herself ever being completely sober, she said, "I don't think so. I would never use the term because of its permanence. It's too heavily weighted for me." I have heard this before. For some—even those who barely drink—the term sober is too narrow and too obstructing to fit into. For KC, consuming on occasion and intentionally works, but she wanted to make it a point to say this is what works for her and maybe won't for others.

Speaking to KC was a breath of fresh air for many reasons. She was open and honest about her alcohol consumption a few years back and how it affected her. She was educational on how she made measurable changes in her lifestyle to uphold her why—her commitment to herself and the community she has connected with because of it. She did not hold back at all in sharing the struggles she has had while saying no to booze and the challenges she has faced when she does drink now that she has made these adjustments.

I related to KC's story and have seen a lot of myself in parts of her journey. It really did make me feel like if she could do it, so could I. I believe that is how a community builds and grows. Like-minded individuals can inspire change within each other and encourage each other with their stories. Her resiliency and commitment to herself were impressive, to say the least, and got me thinking about my own journey.

As we wrapped up, KC said one thing to me I really loved. "Now I consume alcohol like I would dessert. I won't have it all the time, not with every meal, but when I do, I enjoy it."

Such a simple way of framing it, but such a perfect analogy. I will always remember that.

CHAPTER 9:

No

Saying *no* has become one of my favorite responses. In a recent conversation with my best friend David, I realized no became a full sentence for me. "If I've learned anything as I approach thirty, it's that I have no problem saying no. I'm identifying what's not good for me, and I'm saying no more than ever. I have no interest in agreeing to do something or saying yes when internally I am screaming no," I said to him with conviction and genuine joy.

We both stopped and smiled at each other. We have been friends for going on thirteen years. And David has watched me make several mistakes and choose many things that were not good for me. So to express myself this way to him and know that I have been making better choices for myself regularly was a true full-circle moment for me.

"That is so true, Sky. You really have no problem saying no these days, and I am really, really proud of you," he said with the confirmation that I didn't know I needed to hear. Sometimes, a word of affirmation really makes a difference.

Especially when it comes from someone who really knows what you have been through and loves you.

In the past few years, I have practiced saying no repeatedly to things I identify as not in my best interest. I have done so unapologetically, without explanation, and with true confidence. But it's important to note this has not always been the case. In fact, failing to say no to things that do not serve me has created some issues for me in my complex relationship with alcohol throughout the years. I have worked on saying no a lot over the years, and like a muscle, it requires constant exercise. Each time I have chosen to say no to something I know is not good for me, I have watched myself become more confident, stronger, and grounded in my decisions. Each time I have chosen what I need instead of what I may want in the moment, it affirms I am growing in the right direction. It is definitely not easy, but it feels right. It is like choosing my higher self instead of succumbing to instant gratification.

In the past, I have said yes to parties, nights out, trips, and another shot of whiskey more times than I can count. I have agreed to stay out later, ignore my responsibilities, and crack open another bottle of wine because it is what I thought I wanted. I have always wanted to be a go-with-the-flow girl, a fun girl, an outdrink-everyone girl, and I have. Doing whatever felt good at the moment correlated with being a free spirit and being liberated. But it was quite the opposite.

After the fact, I was constantly depleted, angry and disappointed in myself. This happened on a loop. I would agree to stay out past the time I had planned to head home, only to be hungover, exhausted, and depressed the next day and then to do it again the following weekend. It became a pattern I continuously chose for myself. What I had once thought seemed liberating and freeing was now keeping me trapped. All these go-with-the-flow choices kept me in this ugly loop. It was exhausting.

My inner voice was saying no, but I was quick to say yes, for years. And the only one I could blame was myself. Sure, I could blame it on my friend for insisting we order another round of shots or dragging me out of the house for a night at the bar, but ultimately it was me. I constantly found myself agreeing and saying yes to things I knew should be a no for me.

I started understanding that my habits around drinking had a lot to do with the environments I put myself in and my inability to decide to say no. I started asking myself questions: When I decided to have a drink, was it something I really wanted to do, or was I pressured? Did I say yes when I really meant no? Was I compelled to stay out just because everyone else was? Once I answered these questions truthfully, it became clearer to me many of my bad drinking habits centered around my inability to use the word no as a full sentence—whether the no was to friends or to myself. I had failed at doing so, repeatedly. Learning how to be secure enough in my genuine wants and needs took time along with being able to decipher between what I maybe want in the moment and what is actually good for me in the long run. This is a constant work in progress for me, and I still fail at this at times.

Identifying moments where I knew I should say no but chose to say yes anyway has been pivotal for me in shifting my relationship with alcohol. It has also helped shift my relationship with doing what I know is best for me. I have had to do a lot of reflection on moments when I agreed to things that did not serve me. I have had to evaluate those decisions and understand why I chose to say yes in the first place. Again, asking myself important questions was incredibly important to get to the root of it. Why didn't I say no? Why was it so hard for me to say no? What would have happened if I did say no? I have an arsenal of times on which I could reflect, but a few have stood out to me and have helped in my progress.

One of my best friends, who is now a mom and a wife, used to be my partner in crime when it came to drunk days, nights, and weekends. We met in college and have grown up together, seeing each other through lows and highs, and experiencing our true party phase together. As young twenty-somethings, we really did not give much thought as to how our partying and drinking were affecting us. We were young, free, and uninhibited. But as we have gotten older, our partying days have definitely decreased. Like they say, though, old habits die hard.

A few years ago, this friend of mine and I planned to go to brunch. For a majority of people, this lasts for two to three hours max, and then you go home and enjoy the rest of your day. Well, not for my friend and me. The minute I sat down, she had a mimosa waiting for me—champagne and a splash of OJ. She ordered us both bottomless mimosas. I knew this meant I was not walking out of this restaurant without being drunk or very close to it. But I was not complaining. We sat at the bar and made fast friends with a bartender. The bartender was experimenting with drinks and letting us try different concoctions free of charge. We continued accepting every drink she made us, getting exceedingly more tipsy.

Time went by so quickly, between drinking, laughing, and sharing stories. Next thing I knew, three hours had passed in a blink of an eye. Mind you, it was Sunday. Anyone who knows me knows on Sundays I do not make plans. In the past few years, Sundays have become my one day during the week to reset. They usually consist of cleaning my space, meal prepping, getting laundry done, and preparing my to-do list for the upcoming week. And it has been something I have counted on to stay accountable and productive in the week ahead. But on this particular Sunday, I thought, why not?

I had not gotten out of my Sunday routine in a while. This was probably the first moment I should have evaluated whether derailing from my usual Sunday routine would be worth it. Should I have just said no initially, knowing in the past, outings with friends have tended to spill into day drinking? Absolutely. Regardless, I said yes, and at that point, three hours had passed, and we had been drinking with no end in sight.

As we got ready to leave the brunch spot, my friend suggested we take the party to another bar only because the restaurant was closing and we had to leave. "We can't go home now," she said as she already had called an Uber to a bar nearby.

By then, I knew I did not need another drink or to go to another bar. We had already had a great time and drunk enough for one day. Going to the next bar meant more drinks, which meant a hungover Monday and a bad start to my week. But we had been having such a great time, and I really did not want to be a party pooper.

So we took our Uber to the next bar and ordered margaritas and shots. The bar had a happy hour, so everything was half off, which of course meant we ordered multiple drinks for each of us. As I sat at this bar, sipping margaritas with my friend, getting drunker with every sip, I watched my restful Sunday night get farther away from me. Finally, after a few hours, we finally decided to go home.

On my way home in my Uber, I felt immediate regret. Even though it was not too late, I knew I was too drunk and exhausted to accomplish any of my Sunday to-do lists once I got home. See, once you have done this, you can clearly see when you have repeated a pattern you have tried to stay away from. I had fun, but I was disappointed in myself. *Why do you do this? You set yourself up for failure. You don't set boundaries. Now the week is off to a crummy start.*

I repeated this to myself on a loop in my head. Had I chosen to say no a number of times that day, whether to another drink, the next bar, or just to a Sunday brunch altogether, I would have avoided breaking the commitments and routines I had worked hard to keep with myself. Unfortunately, I had done this repeatedly in the past, so even though this was just one day, it appeared like another failure for me.

I had a great time with my friend that day, as I always do. But I knew every time I said yes when deep inside I knew

I should have said no, it made me feel like I had no control over my boundaries that I had worked so hard to put in place with myself. This situation was an eye-opener for me and made me realize I was still choosing people, moments, and alcohol before myself.

Although this situation opened my eyes to my lack of strength in saying no and establishing boundaries, like many things, it takes practice and time to learn enough lessons before we start to enact real change.

It has now been a few years since that brunch turned into an all-day drinking affair. It has taken a lot of practice, mistakes, and more practice to finally listen to my inner voice, which reminds me to set the boundaries that serve me. I am still learning to activate the power in me that is strong enough to say no when I know it is best for me. In all transparency, though, I still misstep from time to time, and I am learning to show myself grace and take these moments as true learning opportunities.

Just a few months ago while visiting my family and friends in the Bay Area, I stayed with my best friend on the last evening of the trip. I had an early flight the next morning, so I explained when I got to his place that I wanted to make sure we did not go to bed too late. Not only did I have to be up for my flight, but I had taken the next day off to tackle some errands and to-dos I needed to take care of. I wanted to be rested enough to take advantage of that day, so I knew I had to set my boundaries aloud from the very beginning.

"No worries at all. We will get to bed at a reasonable hour, and we will be up early so I can take you to the airport," he said reassuringly.

It just so happened that some friends of ours had just moved into a new home a few weeks earlier, so my best friend had the idea to go over there and surprise them since they didn't know I was in town. While that sounded like a great time, I knew we would most likely end up being there late. I knew we would likely have some wine, and I would wake up exhausted and maybe hungover the next day.

Learning from past times and being honest about patterns that show up has been extremely important for me in making decisions, even ones as small as going over to a friend's. I knew what had happened in the past when my friends and I got together after not seeing each other for some time. I knew we were likely to stay up late, have some drinks, and lose track of time. So I knew if we went over to our friend's new home, my next-day agenda was probably out the window.

"It's getting late, so I think maybe we should just stay in, and we can visit them another time. I want to make sure I get some rest before my flight tomorrow. I have a lot to do."

I knew going over there was not the best idea for what I had going on the following day. And I knew I sounded like a party pooper by not wanting to go. See, for everyone else, my list of things to do could wait, and it did not seem like a huge deal. But I knew those things were important for me to get done, and I would regret not doing them. I had already made the commitment to myself to make sure they got done.

I had also failed to go with my gut in very similar situations previously, so I was very clear as to what was the right thing for me at this moment.

As convincing as I tried to be, my best friend assured me we could go for just a bit and be back soon. He promised me we would not stay long and would make it back early enough for me to get some solid rest. I knew he was excited for them to see me, and I also wanted to stop by as well, so I reluctantly agreed.

"Let's come back soon, though." At that moment, I knew that should have been, "You go ahead if you want, but I am going to stay back and rest."

As I presumed, we drove over to our friend's new place, started to have some celebratory glasses of wine, and when I looked at my phone to tell the time, it was 1:30 a.m. We were having a grand time catching up, laughing, and touring the new space. I did not realize where the time went *as usual*. When I realized it was way later than I wanted to be up, I called an Uber for my best friend and me, and we finally made it back to his house. I had to be up in just four hours and already knew I would be exhausted when I woke up. Worse, I knew I would more than likely be hungover and disappointed in myself for agreeing to do something I was hesitant about doing in the first place. As expected, I woke up the next morning groggy and nauseated as I tried to make my way to the airport.

By the time I got home, all I wanted to do was sleep and stay in bed all day. And I did just that. I ran zero errands and did not check a single thing off the list I had made specifically for this day. I remember that day vividly because I was so disappointed and upset with myself. Up until that point, I had felt really good about having exercised my ability to say no and having honored those boundaries I set for myself, so this particular situation really stood out for me. It seemed like a significant setback and regression. *Why do I never learn?* I had to take a step back to remind myself that learning to say no is a work and progress and always will be. What truly mattered was that I took the time to see how I could better set myself up for success next time so it would not happen again.

The times I have failed to say no to drinks, spaces, and people I knew did not serve my best interest have been huge learning pillars for me in my journey to figuring out how to honor my higher self. I keep these moments in my arsenal as references when new opportunities present themselves and I am called to say no. I used to believe these small moments when I said yes to one or a few more drinks or I said yes to a few more hours out were no big deal. But as time has passed and all these small moments have added up, I have realized how significant they have been. Every yes or no I decide on means me being closer or farther away from my most authentic, evolved, and secure self.

In my pursuit to gain a healthy and balanced relationship with alcohol, I realize the only person I can hold accountable is me. I am the only one who can set and uphold these boundaries for myself. Expressing to my close friends and family how important it is for me to say no and to honor the commitments I set for myself has been pivotal in this phase of my life—whether it be drinking less and with more intent or leaving a night out early. Continuing to express how crucial this is for me and then practicing saying no when it comes to anything that does not serve me has helped me on the path to managing my relationship with alcohol in a way that is authentic to me.

I have come to understand the people around you, no matter how much they may care and love you, may not always like the changes that come with you standing your newfound ground, and that is okay. Your new habits, new thresholds, and lifestyles are not always easy for those around you to accept. And that is okay. Those who truly respect you will grow in understanding and will come around. Those who don't may not be for you in the next season. Thankfully, my friends and family have been incredibly supportive as I have grown my strength to exercise saying no repeatedly. It has been far from a perfectly linear journey, and I know there will be times when I may say yes to something I regret. But I am learning to appreciate the moments I can learn from, and I no longer shame myself because of them. No is a full sentence. I have continued repeating that to myself, and it is starting to feel damn good.

CHAPTER 10:

Alcohol and Relationships

Have you ever said something you did not mean when you were under the influence of alcohol? Something you could not take back and regretted greatly? I have on more occasions than I can count. In my history with alcohol, I have noticed getting drunk can result in a number of different outcomes. I have been a happy drunk, a sad drunk, and sometimes an aggressive drunk. Because of the wild card I used to be while drinking, I have gotten into many arguments with those closest to me and regrettably said things I really did not mean. I have strained some relationships with the three people I love the most—my mother, my father, and my former partner. Thankfully, it has been several years since I have had a fight or argument while I have been drinking, and above all else, I have been able to alter my relationship with alcohol and mend my relationships with the people I love along the way.

In my journey to mend my relationship with alcohol and do honest self-work over the past few years, I have had to acknowledge the burden and the effect my use and relationship with alcohol have had on those around me. When I was in the thick of the rollercoaster ride I have had with alcohol as I have grown up, I never really took a step back to understand how my drinking was negatively impacting my relationships and how my coping mechanism was actually hurting me even more because of this. Only when I started trying to better my relationship with alcohol could I face the role alcohol played in some of the worst arguments that have unfolded in my life, and I vowed to change that going forward. The truth is a substance people use for a fun and free time can be the catalyst for damaging important relationships and creating chaos that is not easy to forget.

At this point, you have already read some of my stories and gathered I was a wild teenager and young adult. I have not been the easiest kid to raise, and I know I put my parents through the wringer when I was younger. I have kept them up at night, wondering if I was alive. They have received horrible phone calls in the middle of the night that no parent wants to get, and I have been disrespectful in more ways than I can count. But with all that said, thankfully, I have always had a very close relationship and tight-knit bond with my parents.

As I look back, it wasn't just the sneaking out to get drunk with friends, the lying, or the erratic behavior, but a lot of what I did to hurt my parents over the course of growing up is in some of the arguments we have had. I have never been one to talk back to my mom or dad, scream at them, or say anything out of line, but once I drank and came home from hanging with friends, I could be incredibly out of line. I have behaved in ways that now mortify me and make my soul cringe. Unfortunately, this became a pattern over the years, even into my early twenties.

One time I came home from a very drunken brunch, and I started an argument with my mom. I did not even know what had happened until the next day. She had to recount my behavior to me the next morning. Apparently, I had been swearing and screaming at her for no reason at all. I could not remember why. All I knew was that I felt pure shame and confusion.

Why would I talk so horribly to someone I love? Where was this coming from? How could I display that type of awful character? Was that who I had become? Unfortunately, that is the person I turned into while being drunk on more than one occasion. Even though my mom is one of the dearest and closest humans to me, she has been on the other side of this ugly part of me many times.

One evening, I remember vividly when my mom and I argued, I became so rude and belligerent that my dad had to stop me. He and I exchanged words that still sting and haunt me to this day.

Even though I know I have changed over the past few years, and I have put the work in to avoid getting drunk to the point where I am hurting people I love with my actions, it does not erase these moments. It still affects me to know I have spoken to my parents with disregard and disrespect over the years. We have had many conversations in which I have apologized profusely for my actions and words, and they have lovingly forgiven me since. Even so, I have had to acknowledge it's a part of who I have been.

Regardless if I feel that is not who I am and that the alcohol was inducing it, it has still been me with words that cut like knives. I have had to take full responsibility for that and examine the dark side alcohol can bring out of me. My unstable relationship with alcohol has negatively affected and disrupted the closest bonds in my life. Not only have I suffered because of this, but the people I love most have had to bear the brunt of it.

I was in my last relationship for a full decade, and during that time, he was very much affected by my alcohol use. We got together in our early twenties while trying to figure out who we were and how we wanted to show up in this world. During the ten years we spent together, we went through a lot of ups and downs, as you would imagine a young couple would. We moved through life together as best we could but lacked the tools or awareness to have a truly healthy partnership early on. I battled my demons with alcohol as he had to figure out his.

Together, we did not always create the best combination. We have had many alcohol-induced arguments that could have been avoided had we been sober. I say that now with confidence because once we both worked on our relationships with alcohol and started to make changes individually, we stopped engaging with each other in the detrimental ways we once did when alcohol was the driving force. Before we made adjustments to the way we used alcohol individually and together, it could be something small and insignificant and a bad argument could arise.

I have woken up hungover more times than I can count and could not believe some of the things I said in a drunk argument we had the night before. We repeatedly made the mistake of bringing up unresolved issues while we were drinking together, which almost never went well. An exchange that would have otherwise been a discussion would often end up in a heated argument fueled by booze. Many times I would catch myself thinking, *This did not have to go this way.* But what did I expect when we had both proven that alcohol was at the core of most of our disagreements? It was not about what we were discussing or what the issues were. Instead, it was the tool we were using to unpack them. As counterproductive as it may sound, we did this for years. With very few boundaries surrounding alcohol, we repeated the same behavior in arguments over and over again, yielding me the same results—hurt and regret.

Even though many years have passed since we had an argument like that, the truth is you cannot take things back that have already been said. I know we have both forgiven each other for things said in the heat of the moment when under the influence of alcohol, but I know we both have those memories, and that hurt can still linger. In the process of doing the work to change my relationship with alcohol, I tried to keep those memories at the forefront of my mind, not to punish myself, but to remind myself how alcohol can be a slippery slope for me. Not only does my use impact my life in such a significant way, but it affects the people around me that I care about.

I am incredibly grateful that, even though the relationship ended, we were able to grow into more evolved and mature adults and look back at those arguments as a thing of the past. It's been important for me, though, in and out of that relationship, to do the work individually and acknowledge how my alcohol use hurt and affected my relationship with my partner. Realizing that has helped me to see how alcohol can create chaos and madness within me and around me. Reflecting on things I have said and arguments we have had, although challenging, has been part of the healing process. I know where I have been, and I am constantly working on never regressing or going back there again.

As someone who has struggled with alcohol, I have not only come to understand how alcohol can affect my relationships but also how my relationships can affect my alcohol use. Who we choose to surround ourselves with can impact so many areas of our lives, whether that be our emotions, our health, and our habits. We all affect each other, negatively or positively, which is why I have found it so important not only to continue doing the work internally but to make sure my circle is doing the same. The personal journeys we go through to become healthier and more balanced can be just as important as who our tribe is, as it can directly impact our growth for better or worse.

As I began to make changes in my life to work on my relationship with alcohol, I had to be very vocal about it to the people around me. That was challenging at times but incredibly necessary because I needed my people to understand what I wanted out of life and myself. Along this journey to find a balance and healthy way with alcohol, these are conversations I've continued to have with my family and friends. They have been able to support me in their own individual ways and provide different perspectives that have truly helped me.

This kind of support has looked like holding me accountable by reminding me of what my goals are, being encouraging when I explain what my goals are, joining me for periods of not drinking or drinking only on certain occasions, and being honest with me when it seems I am drifting away from my goals. Support from the people in your life can look and feel all kinds of different ways, but I have found it to be incredibly important in my journey to a healthier me. Who is in your corner matters because they could be propelling you forward or pulling you backward. In either case, the impact could be huge.

Reflection, acknowledgment, and understanding of how alcohol has impacted my relationships have been a big part of my healing and growing process. I have had to look back and face some hurtful and ugly moments when I have said and done things inflicting hurt on some of the people who mean the most to me while under the influence of alcohol. Ultimately, I have had to admit my journey with alcohol has not only taken me on a rollercoaster ride, but it has taken my loved ones on that ride with me, as it so often does for people struggling with substance issues. I also had to come to the conclusion that I wanted to take myself off that ride and take steps to stop putting the people I love through that ride as well.

It can be easy to go through the motions and forget to ask ourselves, *How are my habits and behaviors affecting the people around me, and how are theirs affecting me?* This is of true importance because we are all constantly impacting each other with the way we choose to live our lives. Who you are says a lot about who your tribe is and vice versa, so being intentional about how we show up in our people's lives and being thoughtful in choosing those in our lives is crucial. I have had to be introspective about these elements in my life as I have tried to figure out how to have a healthier relationship with myself, alcohol, and the people in my life.

This work has taken a lot of heavy lifting and involved looking at myself in the mirror with honest eyes. It has been a lot of trial and error, and I am still very much learning every day. Thankfully, forgiveness is a gift people I have hurt along my journey have extended to me, and I have had to learn how to forgive myself in the same way. I am infinitely grateful my family and friends have stood beside me as I have navigated my way out of an often-tumultuous cycle with alcohol. My biggest hope is they can experience a better and more evolved version of me and see the efforts I have made in putting that behind me.

From my experience, alcohol and relationships can play such a huge role with one another, and it all starts with asking ourselves hard but important questions. So if you have or do struggle with alcohol, I encourage you to ask yourself, *Has my alcohol use affected the people in my life? How have the people around me influenced my consumption?*

CHAPTER 11:

Miles—Learning Compassion

———

One of the main purposes of writing this book for me has been to open up the conversation on the role alcohol plays in our different lives and how we can use our stories and experiences to learn, grow, and find more balance. I ultimately hope the stories I shared from my own life, as well as those from interviews I conducted, can help people feel seen and understood. These interviews and experiences others shared with me impacted my growth and shed light on how multifaceted our journeys with alcohol can look. Our path to recovery or a better relationship with alcohol can look different, but there is power in learning from each other and the stories we live.

I sat down to speak with a friend of a friend named Miles and to have an eye-opening conversation embodying the struggles many of us have battled with in silence. I came in contact with Miles through a mutual friend who told me he thought it would be a great idea for us to speak about the topic of my book and, again, open up the conversation regarding alcohol, addiction, and recovery. Our mutual friend knows the full breadth of my story and struggles intimately, so I knew if he suggested we talk, it would be meaningful and important to the framework of my mission for this book.

My conversation with Miles provided a different perspective than any of my other interviews. Little did I know our conversation would bring up a lot of emotions from my own past. Miles told me his story in a raw, genuine, and uninhibited way—the only thing I can ask from anyone I talk to.

The conversation I had with Miles was unique in that I knew very little about him before we spoke. When we know parts of people's stories, we can easily start to fill in the blanks and make assumptions before we get to know them firsthand. So to begin this conversation with a clean slate and allow him to tell me his story for the first time excited and intrigued me. Miles started the conversation by telling me about himself and how alcohol came into his life.

"Trauma was the gateway for me," he explained as he looked back on why he started drinking alcohol. I have heard many different stories about how people begin their drinking journeys. Peer pressure from friends when they are young or trying to fit in during a party phase, or pain and trauma early on in someone's life can lead to experimenting with alcohol. I have seen the way trauma can form a gateway and catalyst for using substances.

Miles grew up in a small town in the South where he got into trouble for growing weed and had to go through a program to quit, eventually leading him to drink more. He explained his drinking then did not last long because he ended up purposely wrecking his car and getting shipped off to rehab in Texas. He stayed sober for seven years after this life-altering event. He shared he spent the majority of his twenties sober and took his sobriety very seriously during that time.

"I definitely went to a lot of meetings and had friends in AA, and it was like the central part of my life for most of my twenties. Frankly, I think it's what I needed at the time—that kind of black-and-white view of the world. I also needed the community, and it allowed me to get through my undergrad and form really deep relationships, get started on my career, and ultimately start grad school," he explained.

After having such a rough start with drinking and going to rehab early on in his life, it made sense that he took his sobriety and commitment to it so seriously. Miles reiterated to me that he found real comfort and aid in AA to support his life during his twenties, a time when many people enjoy partying most. This is a testament to every story being different. How you are in one part of your life does not necessarily determine the next. During his time with AA, Miles found community and a framework to live by. This helped him accomplish many goals he had set for himself. That way of life served him back then, and he grew used to living the life of a sober man. Things changed for him when he turned thirty and decided to start dabbling in drinking again. Miles had started graduate school at the very beginning of his thirties and was making new friends, going out to parties and bars, and dipping his toes in by enjoying drinks in social settings.

"I was getting into being a party boy. Doing a lot of online dating, going out frequently with friends to bars, and just having a lot of really good times," he said with a smile I could hear through the phone.

I could tell Miles looked back at that time as a good part of his life. He enjoyed his freedom and his friends, and he expressed he did not think anything was wrong with his lifestyle at that time. Even though he had started drinking again after being sober for so long, things seemed right to him. He had been keeping up with his studies and handling his responsibilities, and he had great relationships around him. I think it is important to note just because you or someone around you has struggled with alcohol does not mean it's all been bad, or that genuinely good times did not exist. Understanding that can shed light on why people go through ups and downs with alcohol and may even choose to drink again after bad experiences.

When we have great times with our friends, drinking wine and engaging in beautiful conversations, that can be something we crave internally. The question arises: *Is it the friends, the drinks, or the environment we long for?* Maybe it can be a little of all three. But it is easy to equate drinks with a great time. From what Miles described, he enjoyed the person he was at that time—a charming, outgoing, and engaging guy navigating his life as a *new drinker*. At that time, everything seemed to be going right. Miles made the most of his social life while also keeping up with his goals and day-to-day.

However, things started to take a turn in his life. I asked him if he could pinpoint what caused things to go left when it all appeared to be going in his favor. "I think when I started drinking again in my early thirties, I didn't suffer any bad consequences. I completed grad school, kept friendships, and moved forward in my life. Even though partied a lot."

He was confident in his alcohol consumption because everything appeared okay around him, and no negative consequences had surfaced. I have seen this with others and myself in the past, where I loosen the reins on my drinking because I believe I am handling my consumption well, and I feel in control. But I have seen firsthand how quickly things can change when no intentions or boundaries are set with alcohol.

A few years into drinking and having the time of his life, Miles realized maybe the relationship he had with alcohol was going from fun to dangerous fairly quickly. "One day, I thought it would be a good idea to have a drink before work. And up to that point, I had occasionally been ducking out to get lunch at the brewery around the corner from my office and having a couple of beers. Slowly, alcohol was sort of moving earlier in the day and was becoming a habit at that point."

I know to some people, this alone may be shocking, but I can tell you that alcohol can be an incredibly slippery slope when you are not paying attention to your habits, intentions, and overall consumption. What we start to do repeatedly, be it healthy or not, can start to be normal and routine, and we can start running on autopilot. We may not realize what we are actually doing and the habits we are creating. I know this because I have done this. A few glasses of wine one night can easily turn into a few glasses a few nights a week. Next thing you know, you cannot remember the last time you went an evening without even one glass of wine.

After a year of this, Miles knew he needed to get some help. He sought out a therapist in hopes of redirecting his life and gaining some balance. The therapist encouraged him to seek out treatment like AA and focus on abstinence. But the thought of going back to AA, even though he once found community and guidance in that program, no longer felt right to him.

"I was resistant because I thought the AA phase in my life was behind me. I don't know how much exposure you've had with that program, but it's hard to go back to that after you've stepped away for so long."

He explained after being sober for a long period and then having a few years of using alcohol to an extreme point, going back to AA seemed daunting. However, after realizing he needed things to change, he eventually caved, went through a few treatment programs, and tried AA again.

Miles admitted he yo-yoed with drinking on and off at this point, with periods where he would be completely sober and then spiral again. He realized the framework he used to get help was all built from one very binary and one-dimensional model that no longer worked for him.

"I know now there are aspects of the program that are quite triggering for my particular trauma, and I just can't do it over the long term."

Miles and I discussed a lot of the shame-based language the AA treatment program often uses and how it can be triggering and damaging to some. We discussed how much language matters and the way we frame our struggles, our addiction, and the way we talk to ourselves has a lot to do with how we are able to heal and recover. Miles shared how going back to AA and similar treatments dug him deeper into the hole in some ways and made recovery even worse. I realized despite our efforts, sometimes what we think will be the solution can ultimately end up being counterproductive.

Miles was incredibly honest about the struggles he has had with alcohol in the past few years, trying to figure out what works for him and what doesn't. He shared that specific things can lead to his drinking going in the wrong direction. "I've been in this place before numerous times where I sort of leave it all behind, and then something happens. Whether it's stress or something good happens and I want to celebrate, or I am alone and want to decompress. It can open the door back up," he said with sadness in his voice.

If you have ever struggled with alcohol, the smallest things can bring you back into a dangerous space. I know for myself stress and anxiety used to be a big trigger for me and could easily lead down a road of heavy drinking. Because drinking may have gotten you through some tough times, it can be easy to want to rely on alcohol as a way to survive. And just the same, if you associate good times with drinking, it can be instinctual to want to pick up a drink when it is time for a celebration.

When I asked Miles where his current relationship with alcohol stands, he shared an approach I think many of us forget to tap into. When we relapse, or maybe even break a month we have committed to being dry, it can seem like the end of the world. It can translate as failure. He explained he is trying to shift his views on these moments in a way that contributes to his long-term recovery.

"Nowadays, I try to approach my struggles with alcohol with more self-compassion than ever before. Obviously, I know something is going on internally. I have the need in moments to pick up a drink. And maybe that wasn't the healthiest coping skill, but that doesn't mean I need to keep it going. And it doesn't mean I've failed completely and am a bad person."

I completely understood where Miles was coming from. So often, we believe when we have a misstep, we fail and are failures. That negative self-talk can be incredibly destructive and even lead to continuing with behavior you can redirect. Just because we fall off the wagon does *not* mean we have to stay off it. The way we label ourselves and the shame we bestow upon ourselves when we misstep can create a bigger mountain than we were climbing before. It can cause more depression, more angst, and dig us into a deeper hole than was there to begin with. Compassion for ourselves as a starting point to me is a missing link that we are often overlooking in recovery and finding a healthy relationship with alcohol.

Miles explained he does not believe in giving himself a free pass if he has a misstep with drinking. However, he puts his energy into giving himself grace, examining what is happening at the time to learn from it, and understanding himself better. He did not shy away from discussing the heavy struggle alcohol can still be for him. I think that is the case with many of us who have struggled with forms of alcohol addiction, and I believe it is essential to acknowledge that alcohol may *always* be a challenge.

He explained if he does derail off his path, he won't let it be the end of his world. Instead, he plans to take his missteps as an opportunity to learn more about the trigger and how to deal with it differently next time.

It may be easier to tell others to take each mistake as a lesson or opportunity. But using that as the framework for ourselves can be the starting point of a healthier relationship with not only alcohol but self. Miles made it a point to talk about perspective. We discussed how many people tend to think a moderation management or harm reduction approach can be a free-for-all or an excuse to act without real consequences. "I think this sort of harm reduction model is really the only way because it is not giving you blanket permission. It's not saying do whatever you want. But it is also not saying you must quit this forever or you are gonna die. The approach teaches us to be compassionate with our view of the addiction, the behavior, and ourselves."

The way we approach addiction or a battle with a substance has everything to do with how successful we can be in managing it. Miles's perspective homed in on a method I believe can help many people carrying heavy shame and are used to viewing themselves in a negative light because of their struggles. It is not an excuse to make a mistake or keep your foot off the pedal but a reminder that when you fall, you can keep on going. It allows space for the belief there is light beyond the darkness that is right now.

Miles explained the heaviness he has carried around for years and the commitment he has made to himself to step away from it, "If you struggle with substances, you can't help but feel like something is wrong with you. So now I tell myself, *no*. I went through a lot, I have some wounds, and I'm carrying around some difficult stuff. Now I found this way of coping with it. It doesn't help all the time, but I try more and more these days to love that part of myself that historically, I would say is destructive."

This is not always an easy thing to do. Loving all the parts within yourself—the most beautiful parts along with the scary parts—can be extremely challenging. It is a lifelong pursuit that we have to work at constantly. I cannot say there has been a day where I loved every single part of me, but I am working on that each day. I have thought about all the times I have regressed with my drinking, and I fed my mind the most negative self-talk I could think of. This has led to isolation and self-destructive behavior over the years. That approach kept me stuck, ashamed, and embarrassed. These emotions have been the most dangerous for me because they kept me suffering in silence. At times I focused on being down. I was neglecting the lessons I could actually learn from that could keep them from reoccurring.

If you struggle with alcohol or battle full-blown addiction, you probably have an idea of where you envision your best life to arrive one day. When you close your eyes, ask yourself: *What does that look like? What does it feel like? Who are you with? Are you able to maintain a healthy and balanced relationship with alcohol, or are you sober?* I love these questions because making that vision clear to yourself is so important in mapping out your intentions and your path to the life you have in your mind's eye.

When I asked Miles this, he said his wish would be to have "a complete neutrality around all substances." He also was honest about the fact it may never happen for him. "The sort of programming for addiction is within me, and the associations are so strong in my brain between having a drink and pleasure, even though I have suffered a lot because of it."

Whether it be nurture or nature, whether his addiction comes from his environment and upbringing, or if it is biological, it is still something within him. That can be challenging to reprogram and almost impossible for some to shift completely.

He then went on to share that ultimately and realistically sobriety would be his ideal. "I would hope to be completely abstinent and also completely happy being completely abstinent."

So many parts of my interview with Miles resonated with me in a way that I was not expecting. I think that is the beauty of these conversations. I always walk away with something important to think about that I had not anticipated. And as someone who started drinking very young, his story was completely different from my own. Miles went through his twenties as a completely sober man, a time when most people, me included, were experimenting and pushing their boundaries. His life shifted as his relationship with alcohol did in his early thirties, which some may say is a time when consequences are heavier. As he got to know himself and his new relationship with alcohol, he ultimately realized that alcohol was a very slippery slope for him—something I could very much relate to.

Something that stuck with me was his experience and view of treatment and AA. That view shifted from his twenties to his thirties until he came to a conclusion that a program and framework that once really worked for him no longer fit into his life in the same ways that it used to. I truly believe that is why treatment and recovery should have a multidimensional approach. Not only are we all wired differently, coming from an array of backgrounds, experiences, and traumas, but we are also evolving with age and time. What works at one point in our lives may not always be the solution or catch-all.

As time has passed and Miles has tried to manage his relationship with alcohol, his approach has shifted to one of compassion, understanding, and learning. He focuses on shedding the shame that once held him back. I hope Miles's story and his current approach to recovery and alcohol are something we can all learn and ultimately gain from.

There is no one-size-fits-all solution. Different stages in our lives call for different measures. If we can approach our setbacks as opportunities and meet ourselves with compassion, as we might for someone we love, we could all vastly benefit. What can we all learn from our struggles, addiction, and mistakes? Wherever you are, meet yourself with empathy and space to grow from your misstep because *you cannot love yourself and hate your experiences.*

CHAPTER 12:

The Abstinence Myth

Have you ever come across a piece of content that stopped you in your tracks? Whether it be a poem, a book, a song, a YouTube video, or a podcast, and that piece pulls you in and demands your attention. You connect with it, and instantly you know it's something you will never forget. In my constant pursuit to find content around alcohol consumption, I came across a YouTube video on Dr. Adi Jaffe—a #1 best-selling author and doctor known for his book entitled *The Abstinence Myth*. He is recognized as an expert on mental health, addiction, and relationships. The YouTube video is hosted by Ria Health, who interviews Dr. Adi Jaffe about his alternative views on addiction, recovery, and shame. Jaffe not only shares his perspective on addiction but also openly shares his own story of addiction and how he made it out of it.

Jaffe explains that he became an alcoholic and meth addict in his early college years and ended up selling meth, ultimately leading to his arrest and serving a year of his life in jail. He discusses his outlook and views on alternative recovery in his book *The Abstinence Myth*. The book highlights ideas around shame, the inner work needed to face recovery, and an approach to recovery that dismantles stigma, rules, and archaic beliefs. Jaffe's core perspective surrounds the idea that abstinence as the ultimate foundation and requirement for recovery keeps many from getting the help they need. He likens it to

"telling a quadriplegic the only way they can get physical therapy is if they leave their wheelchair at the door. They're relying on alcohol or opiates, or whatever it is they're relying on, to get through the day" (Ria Health 2018).

To drive this point home, he shares,

"Ninety percent of people with alcohol addiction don't get help" (Ria Health 2018).

In my own struggles with drinking, I have come to the realization that measuring the success of my relationship with alcohol by abstinence is not realistic and is a disservice to me—at least at this time. Maybe there *will* come a time when abstinence and sobriety may be what is right for me. However, I do not believe it is the threshold we should be holding *everyone* to dealing with addiction or wanting to change their relationship with alcohol.

Jaffe's alternative perspective allows for a path to recovery that is not bound to specific rules or regulations. His ideology addresses shame, the issues that lead to addiction, and how to heal the wounds that keep us trapped in bad habits and cycles. His recovery method goes against a one-size-fits-all approach because we are all individuals, struggling differently, using differently, and needing different ways of becoming better individuals and leading better lives. I not only agreed with Jaffe's core beliefs and reasoning on *The Abstinence Myth,* but I finally felt seen within a story and perspective. One that did not entail the traditional route of sobriety as its northern star but one founded on true introspection and self-work.

"Addiction isn't one thing, and it's never been one thing" (Ria Health 2018),

Jaffe explains. He talks about the fact that because we have been led to believe addiction is a disease instead of a set of multiple diseases in the way it affects people, there must be one ultimate cure that fixes all. If we were to treat addiction with one cure, an array of symptoms would go completely untreated and unrecognized. We assume that everyone who suffers from addiction has the same symptoms, same challenges and will be cured and healed in the same way. Addiction can look different for everyone, and so does their pathway to healing and recovery.

For some, addiction can look like drinking heavily every day, and for others it may be less than daily but result in binge drinking. Some individuals' recovery may require professional help, but for others holistic healing and alternative methods may work. For others, unpacking their issues with self-work and the help of friends and family may suffice. In that same way, some people who have recovered from addiction to alcohol may choose to drink a bit on occasion while others may find that complete sobriety and abstinence is the best way for them. It truly is not a one-size-fits-all. As a collective, we have to allow room for more than one way, one answer and one way of being. Alcohol addiction and addiction as a whole have shown themselves to be multifaceted. And to treat it like it's a one-dimensional disease can be harmful and worse, keep people from getting the help they need.

A research study that Jaffe conducted at UCLA highlights that only 10 percent of people get help for addiction. He discusses four main hurdles that he has observed keep people from getting treatment for their addiction: cost, logistics, shame, and abstinence. One hurdle that called out to me was shame. I have found that during my challenging times with alcohol, I felt a lot of shame, guilt, and embarrassment that held me back from speaking about what I was going through. I can absolutely see how it would be a big roadblock that could keep people from reaching out for help.

"Addiction is still so looked down upon even with one hundred years of conversation about it. It's one of those things that nobody wants to be forthright about and tell others in their life that they struggle with. So they try to handle it on their own. They try to fix it by themselves, and they dig themselves into a deeper and deeper hole oftentimes" (Ria Health 2018),

Jaffe explains. An abundance of stigma and shame surrounds alcoholism and addiction, which can cripple people into feeling they need to suffer in silence.

Even while writing this book, I have had times where I have felt fear and shame around sharing my story and speaking openly about it. I have had to remind myself that my story empowers me, I am better for my story, and the conversation surrounding alcohol needs to be discussed in an open forum to start dismantling the shame embedded in it. When I struggled with my alcohol consumption, I felt alone. Keeping my story and my challenges to myself only kept me isolated.

I can identify the moment that helped me face my inner demons and realize I needed help—when my father came home from work to take me to the mental health center at our hospital. I had had enough and came completely open about everything that was happening. The fact I let him fully in on what I was dealing with and suffering through liberated me to a degree. It allowed me to hear myself aloud. As a recovered addict himself, my father was able to speak and listen to me with kindness, compassion, and empathy. He held space for me to speak my truth without the crippling fear of shame and ridicule. How much more and how many more people could reach out for the help they are in dire need for if they did not feel the shame and embarrassment surrounding their struggles?

As I dug deeper into Dr. Adi Jaffe's work, I found his TEDx entitled, "Rebranding Our Shame." He talks about the power in branding, labels, and language. He explains how we use branding as a way to lead us through everyday life—whether it be the car we choose, where to buy clothes, and even how we treat people around us. While this influences us to decide what pair of jeans to purchase, hurting no one, the labels we put on ourselves and others *matter* and can make a huge impact negatively or positively.

In his research study at UCLA, Jaffe proposed a series of questions to understand better why such a huge percentage of people choose not to get help for their addiction.

"I wasn't really surprised, but I was depressed to find out that 75 percent, three out of four of our participants identified shame and stigma or the inability to share their problem with other people as a primary barrier" (Jaffe 2015).

Shame is embedded into specific labels that we as a society have inflicted upon those dealing with addiction. What are the first words that pop into your head when you think of an addict or addiction? For many, labels such as loser, fuckup, irresponsible, and defeated come to mind. These labels can keep people stuck and knee-deep in their pain, keeping them isolated and entrenched in the cycle of addiction.

Jaffe calls attention to this attachment we make to labels and their dysfunction.

"If you're depressed, you just don't get out of bed. If you have ADHD, you do poorly in school, or if you're a drug addict, you leave every other responsibility and you let it fall by the wayside because getting high is the most important thing, and so the reality is that these are simple statements. They make sense. We like attaching simple statements like this, but they're wrong. And there's a cost to that" (Jaffe 2015).

So, what is that cost exactly? By labeling addicts, we automatically attach shame, guilt, and embarrassment to them, keeping people where they are.

While there may be sides of truth to some of the labels we attach to addicts and addiction, people are never one thing all the time. We are evolving, multidimensional and complex beings, which can make having just one cure and answer a problem. Jaffe discusses the nuance of addiction and how limiting it can be to treat everyone under one umbrella, with a one-tract mindset and labeling system.

"We can do the best job we want to in terms of determining causes and underlying reasons for conditions and putting together these labels. But the reality is that mental health as a field is in a constant state of reevaluation and refinement. And these labels are approximations, and so when we deal with people as if we know everything about them, because of a label somebody applied to them, we run a risk of dealing with a concept, not a person" (Jaffe 2015).

A person's need for a successful and lasting recovery today can look different next week. Treating addicts as if they are one and the same is to ignore the many faces addiction and substance abuse can have. This speaks to the importance and impact of labeling, language, and approach to addiction. Then again, we have to think about the ninety percent of people not getting the help they need because of these hurdles. How many more lives could we save or improve if we had more evolved and less stigmatized language and labels around alcohol and addiction?

Abstinence proves to be another big hurdle that inhibits people dealing with addiction or substance abuse from getting help. From my own experience and the stories of others, I have come to the belief that abstinence and sobriety are not the only paths that lead to recovery and a better relationship with alcohol. I did not realize, though, how much of an impediment it can be for people getting help with their addiction. Jaffe's perspective on abstinence does not promote abstinence negatively, nor does it mean that the people he has helped in his treatment facility in the past decade do not become abstinent. In fact, in his Ria Health interview, he shares that,

"Forty to fifty percent of the people who come seeking not abstinence but improvement decide to be abstinent in the end" (Ria Health 2018).

However, Jaffe challenges the idea that you must become abstinent to get help and treatment and that it is the threshold of success in recovery. For many people suffering from alcohol addiction, alcohol can become their lifeline in getting through the day and can be their only way of coping with whatever they may be dealing with. So asking someone in the thick of a storm to let go of what they are using to get by cannot only be triggering but become a huge deterrent from changing their lives. With the removal of abstinence as the gatekeeper to recovery, people can begin to make changes without the gripping fear that if they ever drink again and *fall off the wagon*, they will start from ground zero.

Being accountable does not have to be in direct correlation with abstinence. Eliminating abstinence as the foundation for recovery gives space for people to start where they are without feeling like everything that is holding them together is being taken from them in an instant. Jaffe reiterates this does not mean people do not choose to be abstinent. He explains that once people understand what has happened internally and begin to handle that, many do make the decision to lead completely sober lives. What Jaffe argues is that

"The removal of abstinence as a starting point is a way to get people in the door" (Ria Health 2018).

The analogy he makes sheds light on how it can feel to expect abstinence from the beginning point of recovery.

"There is no other field I know of in the world where you have to commit to the success before getting help. It sounds insane to me, and it sounded insane to me since I started going into the field, but it's a little bit like asking an athlete who wants to learn how to play football at the age of five to be able to throw like Tom Brady in order to be able to practice" (Ria Health 2018).

I finally got my hands on Dr. Adi Jaffe's book, *The Abstinence Myth.* As I knew it would, it expanded my mind and viewpoint on how I and how we as a society frame recovery and addiction. The book poses some important questions on recovery. Is the outcome we are looking for when it comes to treatment just abstinence? Or is it a healed, evolved person who can have a healthy relationship with alcohol—whether that turns out to be abstinence or just healthy moderation? The outcome desired is based on the individual, their background, their coping mechanisms, and layers that cannot be reduced to a singular profile. Jaffe explains,

"When we take some of the spotlight off the addiction, it widens the stage of what's going on and makes recovery, drinking less, and abstinence much more possible, widening your lens" (Jaffe 2018, 48).

The way we look at the problem keeps everyone trapped. Of course, many good treatment centers address additional issues on top of the elimination of drinking. However, so many people who need help won't start the conversation when the only solution that's put in front of them is complete abstinence. Yet the industry persists. This idea of widening the lens was really moving to me because alcohol addiction is so much more than the addiction itself but has so much to do with addressing the inner workings of what is going on inside of us. The idea that abstinence would be the first part of recovery, rather than first getting help to dismantle the issues keeping the individual in addiction, seems backward and counterproductive. As someone who has had times when I spiraled using alcohol, I can say that for me, it had so much less to do with the alcohol than it did with the storm that was brewing internally. It was not until I sat with myself, faced the issues I was battling, and started to learn how to heal those wounds that I could adjust and change my relationship with alcohol and the space it held in my life.

Dr. Adi Jaffe's perspective and methods regarding addiction, recovery, and shame really called out to me and gave me hope that these conversations are out there. It reinforced my belief that recovery and healing are not linear; they are a process that looks and feels different for many. Addiction is complex and cannot be solved with a one-dimensional approach. Such an approach leaves out a huge percentage of people who need the help but cannot face the shame and fear that is often impressed upon them with traditional forms of cookie-cutter treatment. Jaffe's viewpoints address how impactful labeling and shame can be for those suffering from addiction and breaks down the importance of language.

Significant numbers of people are in need of help, and so the question arises—how can we create a way to empower more people to get help and remove those barriers to recovery? Jaffe started IGNTD, a progressive recovery program that serves to eliminate as many deterrents and hurdles that people dealing with addiction face when looking to make lasting changes to their lives. The goal is healthy, healed, and recovered individuals who can make sustainable changes for the better. Whether that be complete abstinence or moderation is not for anyone but the individual to decide. These perspectives certainly have affected me in the most positive way, not only with how I manage my own relationship with alcohol but how I care for those around me who are struggling and my views on recovery as a whole. How much could we all benefit if we abandoned the idea that recovery looks only one way and addiction is just one thing? How many more people could get the help they need?

CHAPTER 13:

Lost in Movement

Many of us who have struggled with dealing with our vices know it can be easy to pick something else up as a vice to substitute for what we are trying to avoid. You see this with alcoholics who pick up smoking cigarettes when trying to get sober, and I have seen it with my dad getting into fitness once he quit drugs. In the latter case, my dad was able to find something healthy to take some space in his life while he worked his way out of his addiction. From my vantage point, this really impacted his life and my family's quite a bit.

Recovery from addiction is not something that should or can be solved by picking up another vice or filling time with another habit. However, I believe finding things you enjoy can benefit your overall well-being and be helpful during and after recovery. A lot of time, addiction can take up a lot of space in an individual's life, and they can get away from doing the things that bring them joy, life, and peace. They may even find that they never made the space to discover things they are passionate about. Watching my dad dive into fitness after recovering from addiction, and seeing how it impacted his mood, health, and overall wellness made me appreciate how much of a tool passion can prove to be.

Although I have never had to battle what many would call full-blown addiction, I have had to work diligently to manage my relationship with alcohol over the years, with many ups and downs. I have tried a lot of different methods in attempting to find balance with how I use alcohol—from detox cleanses, meditation, not keeping alcohol in the house, limiting alcohol to weekends, therapy, and more. During the pandemic, I found something that not only helped me tremendously with my relationship with alcohol but also benefited so many other areas of my life.

The pandemic was an incredibly challenging time for all of us, and consequently a time when many were consuming more alcohol than ever before, me included. I worked from home, stayed home to avoid people, and basically lost my mind. I then got laid off from my tech job and was sinking deeper into my angst and insanity. It seemed totally reasonable to reach for a glass of wine when 2:00 p.m. rolled around because why not? The world was hanging by a thread anyway. To add to that, I was living in a 550-square-foot studio with very little space to move around, and the only exercise I was getting was a short walk around the neighborhood, if that.

Almost a year into the pandemic, I moved to a much bigger apartment with a fantastic gym in the building. This gym ended up becoming my saving grace during this time and has continued to be one of my biggest life savers up until today. This all started about a year and a half ago. Before this, I was a yoyo gym goer. I would go for a few months and then lose steam and stop going for a few months and so on. I can say that before, I never truly took it seriously. I know that now because I had not taken enough time to actually fall in love with working out and movement. Beyond that, I had never really understood or experienced all the incredible effects fitness has on the body and the brain. It was not until the pandemic, when I started going to the gym regularly, that I made it my mission to create consistency and make movement a staple in my routine.

As I became more consistent with my workouts, I realized it to be my favorite part of my routine. We were still in the trenches of the pandemic, and the gym was becoming an oasis and an escape for me. The gym became a place to express myself and release any tension and anxiety. It proved to be a space to recalibrate myself among the chaos that was happening in the world. I noticed how good I felt after working out and how it impacted my entire day. On days I skipped the gym, I was stiff, foggy, irritable, and distracted. But on days when I prioritized my workout, I felt simply alive. Working out gave me emotional, mental, and physical balance. It allowed me to be my best self throughout the day. Although I still had anxiety and the worry of living through a pandemic, I now had an outlet and started to feel a lot more like myself.

As months went by, I began to notice the measurable and direct ways fitness and movement were changing my life and my behaviors surrounding alcohol. I wasn't reaching for that crisp glass of rose at 2:00 p.m. because I had already planned to work out later in the day when my craving for alcohol would start to surface. I would often have the strongest desire and need for a glass of wine (or four) once the day was starting to wind down as a way to decompress and relax. Now I substituted that glass of wine for an intense workout where I could sweat, cry, and let it all out—real decompression. Even if I still craved that glass of wine, I was pushing it until way later in the evening where I would probably only have time for one.

Something I noticed was that many times I was drinking out of boredom. I was laid off, stuck at home, and I never really got into making sourdough like everyone else was taking up during the pandemic. I often drank in front of the TV to pass the time. So I made the gym a place to go and a thing to do whenever that boredom built up. Even when I really dreaded having to go down to the gym and move—and there have been plenty of those days—I always without a doubt felt so much better when I was done. I also noticed that as my consistency in the gym grew, my desire for alcohol started to change. From my perspective, I was working out and taking care of my body, so I did not want to "ruin" my progress or efforts with a glass of wine or cocktails. I found that my habits surrounding alcohol were more intentional if I was working out regularly.

Stress has also been a big reason why I have been compelled to drink in my past and has served as a coping mechanism I have used throughout my life in order to relax and be more at ease. As fitness became more of a priority in my life, I realized how movement was aiding me and serving as a tool for me to manage my stress. When I noticed I was uneasy and stressed out, I would hop on the Peloton bike or lift some weights, and I would notice how, after my workout, I felt instantly better. My stressors were not gone by any means, but everything started being more manageable when I was moving and sweating regularly.

I had now found a coping mechanism that did not involve finishing a bottle of wine by myself. I had found something that empowered me, strengthened me, and gave me more control of my life. Working out was taking a place in my life that, contrary to alcohol, I could feel good about after. It did not make me forget my worries like alcohol can sometimes do, but it made me actually more aware. Something about making a conscious and repeated decision to better myself, in this case in the form of physical fitness, really opened my eyes to the power I had within me. Because if I could be intentional enough to make decisions that are good for me, I could be intentional enough to make better decisions around the things that do not serve me.

My intention is surely not to promote fitness as the catchall solution to addiction, recovery, or any negative habits when it comes to alcohol because it is not. I do not believe one thing can solve these struggles or serve as a placeholder for what alcohol or any other substance has played in an individual's life over time. We cannot aim to solve addiction or overcome our recovery as a whole by substituting vices or distracting ourself with another tool or hobby. But I can share from my experience, in my long pursuit to attain a healthier, more balanced relationship with alcohol, that working on my body and making movement a priority has been a godsend in more ways than one. I reacquainted myself with fitness and the multitude of benefits it brings during a time when I was drowning along with the rest of the world.

Before I took fitness seriously, I was drinking more than I had in a while and loosening my boundaries around alcohol. I was rationalizing it, though, because…well… it was a pandemic, and everyone was seemingly in the same boat. But when working out regularly started to be a priority, it quickly became my safe space, which made me more aware of my relationship with alcohol as a whole. Slowly, I realized how maintaining consistency with my workouts was impacting my choices when it came to drinking. My commitment to taking care of my body through movement had a strong and direct correlation with my decision-making with alcohol.

Everything started to connect. If I worked out, I did not have the need to drink a lot or at all. I made movement a priority over sitting in front of the TV with a glass of wine. I was more aware and particular with what I put into my body—alcohol included. I used exercise instead of alcohol to cope. If I had worked out, I could be more intentional throughout the day. When I got serious about the gym, I had no idea the ways in which it would have an impact on my relationship with alcohol or that it would have an impact at all. I did not start with the hopes of attaining any of which I have shared, but I did it because I knew I needed something to balance the stress, anxiety, and rollercoaster that the pandemic had served us all on a platter. I desperately wanted to feel good about myself, but little did I know the gift that fitness would continue to give me.

I have continued to work out and stay consistent in the gym over the past year and a half. It is not always the easy thing to do, and I didn't always have the motivation to do so. It has not solved all my issues with alcohol or created the perfect balance in my life. There is no one solution, but it is one tool I am committed to and will never give up. Some weeks I do not make it as much as I would like to, but the goal is to stay committed and never give up. I have the same outlook in pursuing a healthy relationship with alcohol.

I know I am not perfect and very much a work in progress, but what I do know is I dedicate myself to continuing working on my relationship with alcohol, and I am never going to give up in trying to become the healthier version of myself. I have seen the way moving my body on a constant basis has altered my mind, my emotional well-being, and my physical form while it has subsequently helped me in managing and improving my habits around alcohol. I have seen firsthand how everything we choose to do connects with each other. Beyond the dopamine, serotonin, and endorphins we can produce from exercise, I have gained perspective, balance, commitment, and consistency.

I consider these things absolutely priceless. They are things I apply in my present everyday life that I could not have dreamed of getting from deciding to get my butt to the gym regularly. I am infinitely grateful for the power of exercise and the role it has and continues to play in my life and journey with alcohol. So I encourage you to start where you are, start moving, commit to it and yourself, and get *lost in movement* with me.

Conclusion

A few weekends ago, I attended Pride in San Francisco. It is the first time I have been in years. I went with a ton of good friends who had been planning this for months, so it was something we all looked forward to. A lot of these friends I have known for more than a decade. They have seen me through many of the challenging times and experiences you have read about in this book. They have watched me struggle through some of the most hopeless, darkest, and scariest moments of my life and have known all the many faces of my struggles with alcohol in the past years of our friendship. They have also seen me achieving, excelling, and applying the lessons I have learned in more recent years.

Because I live in Los Angeles, traveling back to the Bay Area where I was raised and seeing all my friends is always a celebration. Often celebration means raising glasses and drinking, and lots of them. This Pride felt significant for me because it was the first time I was going to be with these friends in quite some time. While I was really looking forward to seeing them and having a great time, I was pensive about how much alcohol was going to be involved all weekend. To be honest, I was worried about my own drinking. I have done my best to be more intentional and aware of my alcohol consumption in the past few years, and a lot of times I keep my commitment to myself. But admittedly, at times I have reverted back to old habits.

I felt good about going to Pride and confident in my ability to maintain my intentions with drinking with serious moderation all weekend. I thought about it a lot before the weekend arrived. I wrote down my intentions and spoke about them to all my friends. I went into the weekend feeling secure and grounded. On each day of Pride, we attended parties and events where they served alcohol in abundance, and on each day, I went in with a game plan on how much alcohol I was okay drinking.

I remember being at one of the parties and looking around at everyone laughing, dancing, and having a blast, and I thought, *I do not need another drink. I am happy. I am surrounded by joy, and it is just not necessary.* These were new thoughts for me. In the past few years, as I have worked on maintaining a healthier relationship with alcohol, I have exercised drinking less and in moderation. But there have been times when I have negotiated with myself: *It's just one more drink.* I have both given in and stuck to my guns. But the point is, this knee-jerk reaction lives inside of me that says, "I want more," when it comes to alcohol.

That party during Pride stood out to me because that voice was saying something different this time around. It was a small moment, but it made me aware of the work and the time it took for me to get to where I am today. The therapy, the self-reflection, the lessons learned and applied, and the relentless pursuit to grow are all embodied in one simple moment. This carried on throughout the weekend, and the more I thought about it, the less I wanted to drink. I felt stronger, in control, and *proud of myself,* and that was really big for me.

As I continue examining my relationship with alcohol, getting to know myself better, and applying the many lessons I have learned, one thing I know is true—this is a never-ending journey that will always be a work in progress. As you now have read, my journey with alcohol started when I was very young, at the green age of fifteen. It has been a part of my life now for a decade and a half. For some, it might seem like I should have it figured out by now, and I cannot deny there are days when I feel like that as well. But I know we never truly have it "figured out."

As a youth, I moved recklessly and with very little awareness. I chased adventure, excitement, and experience to the fullest, and boy did I live that. I also lived the many consequences of my choices: broken teeth in a club fight, a rocky relationship with my parents, and horrible mornings after being drunk while hitting several rock bottoms along the way.

Along this journey, I have had to look at myself in the mirror and face self-reflection I honestly thought would take me out. But it did *not.* I have learned, I have regressed, and then I have gotten back up again. *Over and over.* I have utilized therapy, fitness, the support of close friends and family, meditation, and moderation management. And one thing I have learned throughout this process is that none of these things will work if you do not work. It takes *constant* work to keep your foot on the pedal and not fall back into old habits. It takes *constant* work to remember *your why* and keep your intentions. It takes *constant* work to look in the mirror and be honest about where you are. It takes work to understand what is or has caused the struggles you have with alcohol. It all takes effort. You have to be willing to do this arduously and relentlessly for a healthier relationship with alcohol. But I am here to tell you there *is* light outside of the darkness that you may have felt or are currently feeling.

If there is anything I hope to put out into the world through this text, it's that recovery and attaining a healthy relationship with alcohol is not a one-size-fits-all approach. For some, sobriety can be the foolproof answer to their prayers, and others may not feel the need for complete abstinence in order to lead a healthy and balanced life. Because addiction and struggles with alcohol can have many layers, healing and recovery should be approached with a multifaceted perspective and method.

Measuring our relationships with alcohol by sobriety may not be the best indicator for all. We have to be willing to break free from archaic belief systems that may be keeping many from getting the help they need. By allowing for more than one answer to issues with alcohol, we create more space for recovery and are able to treat a wider range of symptoms that could otherwise be ignored. Healing and recovery are not one-dimensional, and neither should our approach be. As I have mentioned, I do not have it figured out, and I am still learning about how to have a healthier relationship with alcohol, but what I do know for sure is that I am lightyears from where I was even one year ago. I stopped measuring my progress by solely using sobriety as my apex and goal, and I started leaning into learning, honesty, moderation, and consistency. This allowed me to get to where I stand today—a work in progress committed to growth and a healthier approach to drinking.

I wrote this book to demystify the stigma around addiction, discuss awareness surrounding alcohol and addiction, and help provide perspective on creating healthier habits surrounding alcohol. I have shared the many ups and downs I have encountered with alcohol and the ways in which I am finding my way to a healthier and more balanced relationship with myself and alcohol, along with the stories of others who have had their own unique battles with alcohol, in hopes that they provide a space for you to feel seen, heard, and connected. I have read stories that feel so far from my own reality and have left me discouraged because I do not model what I have seen recovery *should* look like. I hope this text serves as the opposite for you.

I hope you see yourself through my stories and see that the light at the end of the tunnel is on the other side of the work you are more than capable of. Most importantly, I hope it moves you to start carving your path and defining what a healthier relationship with alcohol looks like for you. I encourage you to start owning your experiences and stop letting them keep you in shame. In the process of writing this book, I have learned the power of sharing my stories and the strength in having gone through them. We are more powerful when we are sharing our experiences and the resources and tools that have helped us along our journey. Let us open the conversation on alcohol abuse, addiction, recovery, and everything in between, and let us gain information and education to better support each other. I know you will go on to find your *undiscovered lighthouse*.

Acknowledgments

___

If you are reading this, you have likely read all of *An Undiscovered Lighthouse*, and for that I want to extend my deepest gratitude and thanks. My biggest purpose in embarking on the journey of writing this book was to share my story, and in doing so, provide content surrounding alcohol, addiction, and shame that could make others struggling feel seen, heard, and understood. So thank you for allowing me to share my story with you in the most raw and open way I can. Thank you for lending me your time and attention and taking in some heavy moments of my life.

I started writing this book during my thirtieth year on this earth, and it has been the most transformative year of my life to date. Because of that, completing this project has been one of the hardest things I have had to do. During this year while writing this book, my relationship of ten years came to an end, and with that came many big life changes. I have had to start over in a lot of ways and figure out a new path that often felt like an impossible Rubik's Cube. I say all this to say that it has taken everything I have to get this book in your hands today, and I am eternally grateful that you decided to pick it up and give it a chance.

This book would not have come to fruition without the constant and unwavering support of the incredible people I call my friends and family.

I won the parent lottery with my mom and dad, and to you both, I am all the good things I am because of you. You have never stopped showing up for me, believing in me, supporting me, holding me up, and building me up, even when I know it was *not* easy. You have equipped me with the tools I needed and used to become the woman I am today. You have stood by, in front, and behind me, every step of the way. I can never express enough thanks for who you have been and continue to be for me. This book is for you and for us. Forever, thank you.

Silas, I will never forget all the years we talked about this becoming a reality and all the moments you encouraged me to take a chance on myself. You have championed me, encouraged me, and given me the push I have needed more times than I can count. You have been there for a lot of these stories. You have been there for a multitude of highs and lows, and still, you have always loved me and seen the higher me. For allowing me to share parts of our life and story together, thank you. For holding space for me when I second-guessed whether I could do this, thank you. For the lessons we have learned together, thank you.

To my eternal best friend David—you have been the rock, the shoulder, the sounding board, the confidant, the safe place, and the family I have needed for over a decade but especially the last year. You have always seen the woman I could be and have invested in my growth like no one else. You have been my unpaid therapist and have given me advice that I will always carry with me. You have also been present for so many of these stories, and you have been there to help me through them. You have caught me when I have fallen and built me back up, over and over. You show up for me, whether for celebration or heartache. You show up the way no one else can. This book, in large part, stems from so many of the conversations we have had. Thank you for being here, always.

To my Lola, thank you for believing in me and always being such a badass grandmother. Your example as a strong independent woman who has succeeded in the face of obstacles has inspired me and reminded me where I come from. Your investment in me and my project means the world. Thank you from the bottom of my heart.

To all my other close friends and family who have uplifted, supported, and helped me during the process of writing this book, my biggest thank you. For the phone calls, visits, and words of encouragement while I navigated my way through writing my first book. For understanding when I have been busy or away, and for always believing in my mission, I appreciate you: Jaewynn, Simone, Andrea, Fooms, Tam, Kristian, Dana, Juan, Malik, and Jamin—thank you!

I have to give a huge shoutout and thanks to Eric Koester of the Creator Institute and Georgetown University whose coaching made starting this book a reality. Your energy always provided such a boost of confidence and propelled me forward many times. To the team at New Degree Press and to my editors, Angela Mitchell and Kenneth W. Cain, your guidance and diligent work to get me through my writing and publishing journey had been essential to this project. Thank you.

Over eighty people in my loving community made this book possible by supporting my presale campaign and ordering copies months before they would actually receive them. All your contributions have meant so very much to me. Thank you for your investment in me, my story, and the most important project I have ever worked on. Your belief in me has touched my heart in so many ways.

Aaron Rau
Adriana Rodriguez
Aimee Evan
Alicia Mccool
Andrea Olivares
Ayana Harrison
Ayana Harrison
Betty Rennolds
Caio Rodrigues
Cathy Perez
Claudia Pugay
Consolacion Bergstedt
Craig David
Dana Louise Clarino
Dominique Ellis
Elizabeth Martinez
Eric Koester
Ernesto Palazuelos

Eusi Pease
Felisa Wiley
Gabino Avila
Ian McLeod
Ian Morales
Irene Gardner
Ivania Nand
Ixquel Sarin
Jaewynn Roberts
Jake Pese
Jamai Valentino
Jamin Rodriguez
Jarrett Wright
Jasmine Malone
Johanna Masiclat
Jonathan Burk
Jonathan Sujo
Juan Carlos Boza Morales

Karen Lurry
Karen Vandermeulen
Karla Mooney
Katherine Diaz
Kathy Orozco Molina
Katie Lucas
Katya Davydova
Kelly Gorrell
Kenya Scott
Kimberly Dela Cruz
Kristen Canniff
Kristian Franklin
Kristy Mai
Laura Rieken
Leonor Iparraguirre
Lexi Hilgart
Luis Morales
Maggie Carey
Malik Knox
Michele Barajas
Michelle Panganiban
Miranda Palmer
Nomi Nguyen
Ocean Fine
Orlando Pubill
Robin Lantin
Ron Del Rosario
Rosalind Landless
Sandra Pasia
Sharon Sakai
Simone LB
Stephanie Lansang
Stephanie Lanza
Stephanie Roberts
Summer Harrington
Susan Suarez
Sydnee Morris
Sylvia Mills
Tam Badshah
Tawny DeVore
Terrance George
Utamu Pease
Victoria Cortez
Vincent Valino
Zapata Caroline

To all of those who are reading this and struggling with your relationship with alcohol, the fact that you picked up this book means you are searching and wanting better. I want you to know I see you, I hear you, and I have been there. I hope you find something in this book that pushes you to start the work and put shame behind you. I am thankful that you are here, and I believe you too can find your undiscovered lighthouse.

Appendix

AUTHOR'S NOTE

Andrew, S. 2018. "About 40 Percent of Americans Drink Too Much, Study Says." *Newsweek*. July 18, 2018. https://www.newsweek.com/study-40-percent-americans-drink-too-much-1029294.

Hauck, G. 2021. "Americans are using alcohol to cope with pandemic stress: Nearly 1 in 5 report 'heavy drinking.'" *USA Today*. September 22, 2021. https://www.usatoday.com/story/news/health/2021/09/22/covid-19-pandemic-heavy-drinking-survey-alkermes/5798036001/.

CHAPTER 2: YOU CAN'T LOVE YOURSELF AND HATE YOUR EXPERIENCES

Dykstra, Andrea. 2018. "Quotes to Live By—In order to love who you are, you cannot hate the experiences that shaped you." October 17, 2018. https://inspirationalgoods.com/blogs/live-inspired/quotes-to-live-by-in-order-to-love-who-you-are-you-cannot-hate-the-experiences-that-shaped-you.

CHAPTER 12: THE ABSTINENCE MYTH

Jaffe, Adi. 2015. "Rebranding Our Shame." Filmed July 2015 in UCLA, CA. TED video, 15:11. https://www.youtube.com/watch?v=A9xFJ_hqzDQ.

Jaffe, A. 2018. *The Abstinence Myth: A New Approach for Overcoming Addiction Without Shame, Judgment, or Rules.* IGNTD Press.

Ria Health. 2018. "Ria Health Speaks with Dr. Adi Jaffe about his book, 'The Abstinence Myth.'" Ria Health. December 14, 2018. 40:55. https://www.youtube.com/watch?v=BJP4J-919SM.

www.ingramcontent.com/pod-product-compliance
Lightning Source LLC
LaVergne TN
LVHW010331070526
838199LV00065B/5721